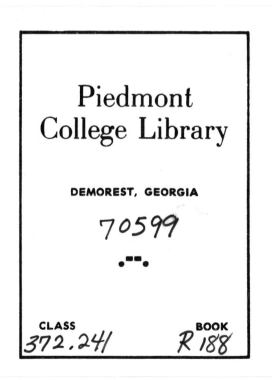

OPEN EDUCATION

OPEN EDUCATION:

the informal classroom

A
selection
of readings
that examine the
practices and principles
of the British infant
schools and their
American
counter-
parts.

Selected and edited by

CHARLES H. RATHBONE

CITATION PRESS, NEW YORK • 1971

Library of Congress Catalog Card Number: 73-173449
Standard Book Number: 590-09505-6

Published by Citation Press, Library and Trade Division, Scholastic Magazines, Inc., Editorial Office: 50 West 44th Street, New York, N.Y. 10036.

Printed in the U.S.A.
Second printing, 1972

Line art by Irmgard Lochner after original drawings by Cornelia Voorhees of the Early Childhood Education Study of Education Development Center, Newton, Massachusetts.

"Two Classrooms" by Anthony Kallet first appeared in THIS MAGAZINE IS ABOUT SCHOOLS, vol. 1, no. 1 (April, 1966). Reprinted by permission.

"Leicestershire Revisited" by William P. Hull was first published by the Early Childhood Education Study, Newton, Massachusetts, as OCCASIONAL PAPERS 1 (1970). Reprinted by permission.

"Messing About in Science" by David Hawkins first appeared in SCIENCE AND CHILDREN, vol. 2, no. 5 (February, 1965). Reprinted by permission of the National Science Teachers Association, 1201 Sixteenth St., N.W., Washington, D.C. 20036.

"Some Thoughts on Integrity" by Anthony Kallet first appeared in PRIMARY SCHOOL BROADSHEET 5, which is published by the Leicestershire Education Department Advisory Section (1967). More recently it appeared in OCCASIONAL PAPERS 2 (1969). Reprinted by permission.

"Some Thoughts on Children and Materials" by Anthony Kallet first appeared in MATHEMATICS TEACHING, no. 40 (Autumn, 1967). It is reprinted here by permission of the British Association of Teachers of Mathematics and the author.

"I-Thou-It" by David Hawkins is the revised version of a talk given at the Leicestershire Primary Teachers' Residential Course on April 3, 1967. It was first published in MATHEMATICS TEACHING, no. 46 (Spring, 1969). It is reprinted here by permission of the British Association of Teachers of Mathematics and the author.

1/11/74 Becker & Tyb 3.85

CONTENTS

PREFACE

"Open education" refers to an educational phenomenon associated with recent reforms in British primary education. Also known as the "integrated day," "Leicestershire model," or simply as the "informal" infant school approach, open education is characterized by certain philosophical principles and certain classroom practices. It is the intent of this collection to present an overview of these principles and practices so that American teachers may better understand this classroom and how and why it operates as it does.

During the past several years, American interest in open education has grown tremendously. While five years ago knowledge of this classroom was practically nonexistent, now nearly every American teacher has read at least one article, somewhere, that describes its operational features. To express this explosion more statistically, in 1968 only thirty articles were published in the United States that even mentioned what was going on in England; two years later there were over three hundred.

Several explanations may be advanced to account for this sharp increase in interest. One is the desperation accompanying American teachers' dissatisfaction with the traditional classroom—a hungry man searches for food more diligently, after all, than one who has been well fed. Another explanation is a simple historical one: The Plowden Report was released in England at the very end of

1966; in the United States Joseph Featherstone's three *New Republic* articles were published in the fall of 1967. Both called immediate attention to the fact that open education classrooms were exciting places in which young children can live and learn.

However, the quality of attention focused on an issue is often more important than the sheer number of articles written about it; and here one must acknowledge the special roles played in the United States by the Elementary Science Study of Newton, Massachusetts, and the National Association of Independent Schools of Boston. ESS curriculum designers, though from the mid-1960's aware of what was happening in England, were apparently too tough-minded and independent to accept the open education approach uncritically. Instead, they began testing its ideas against their own, incorporating what seemed reasonable and relevant, rejecting or retesting the rest. Given their seriousness of purpose, they found little time to sing the praises of open education, and this no doubt delayed its popularization. There was an evident advantage to this delay, however, for when the stampede finally did come, it meant that there was a small group of knowledgeable men and women who had already worked through the problems of implementation—at least in one setting—and who were now in a position to assist others elsewhere.

The National Association of Independent Schools has also contributed significantly to promulgating the basic tenets of open education. For several years now Edward Yeomans, NAIS Associate Director of Academic Services, has organized summer workshops designed to promote an understanding of open education, workshops that have included on their staffs top-notch British administrators and teachers.

Both NAIS and ESS have been reluctant to proselytize, and I think this reluctance is shared by the contributors to this book. Although the authors represented here are unabashed proponents of open education, they are in no way interested in offering recipes for reform. They are proponents of an approach that emphasizes trust, freedom of choice, flexibility, and individual responsibility—not just for children but for teachers and schools as well. While open education constitutes no fixed "system," it does anticipate that each teacher will come to know his own philosophy and, acknowledging it, will then seek to work out an appropriate methodology. This requires—for open education teachers as well as for readers of this book— an ability to be selective and critical of whatever new ideas come along. In this process of decision-making, the teacher learns to capitalize on his own strengths and to reconfirm certain of his own beliefs, while learning at the same time to recognize his own weaknesses and to test out new ideas, whatever their source.

This, I believe, is the way realistic and responsible change occurs in schools: one by one, individual classroom teachers begin to take responsibility for who they are and how they teach and what goes on within their classes. Teachers—even competent, experienced ones— become dissatisfied with what they are doing and begin looking for new ways. Often change is gradual and pragmatic. A teacher may begin to experiment in one area of his teaching, perhaps in art or creative writing, and later, while trying to stimulate a similar energy and enthusiasm for some other area, will employ analogous techniques. In this way a freer, more integrated approach to teaching can spread from subject to subject—or from Friday afternoon activities to Monday morning. The precise nature of these changes depends, of course, on the particular teacher, school, curriculum committees, children, and so on, but the point is that growth *does* occur, teachers and schools *do* change, and life for children in classrooms can become less formal and more natural.

Personally, I do not believe there can ever be one right way to change or one right way to teach. One of my most vivid memories of a recent visit to England is of two totally different teachers working side-by-side in a Leicestershire infant school. (In England, "infant" schools are for children of ages five through seven, while "junior" schools are for eight- through eleven-year-olds; the term "primary" school refers to a school combining infants and juniors.) One was as informal, libertarian, and absolutely steeped in open education as anyone could imagine; the other was quite traditional but obviously first-rate within that framework. Somehow between the two—and between them both and their headmaster—they had built enough mutual respect to permit each to go her own way in strength and in confidence. It is this ability to acknowledge and honor the uniqueness of individuals that is at the heart of open education; each article of this book will, in its own way, make this point.

In assembling this collection and in putting together my own thoughts about open education, a number of people have been of help. So thanks: to Maurice Belanger, Courtney Cazden, Dave Purpel, and Roland Barth for their respective roles in helping to clarify the meanings of open education; to the staff of the Elementary Science Study for graciously opening its files to me as I searched for bibliographical materials; to Pat, my wife, to Bill Hull, and to Allan Stone, who each helped me gain some sense of where I stood in relation to the philosophies of this movement; to the authors of these articles for their permission to publish them in this collection; and finally to innumerable teachers on both sides of the Atlantic for inviting me into their classrooms to observe, ask questions, take notes, and teach.

C.H.R.
June 1971

INTRODUCTION

by John Holt

By 1962 or so, like many other teachers, I had come to realize that the things that teachers customarily do in class, and that I had been doing, were not only *not* helping students but were doing almost all of them active and serious harm. The question was, what to do instead. It seemed clear that fear was the enemy of learning and equally clear that there is no way to make someone learn something you have decided he ought to learn without making him afraid of what may happen to him if he does not learn it. From spending much time with them, I had observed that babies and little children, before the adults around them began trying to direct and control and force their learning, were independently, resourcefully, tirelessly, and very capably learning on their own. Perhaps, then, the thing to do was to try to make schools places where children could go on doing what they most wanted to do and had already been doing—move out into the world of human experience around them and in their own way learn to act in it, cope with it, and make sense of it.

The trouble was that I, again like many other teachers, had almost no idea how to do this, or what such schools and classrooms might be like, or what the children would do there, or, most important, what *I* would do there. And

1

so more and more of us began to make trips to what seemed to be an educational New World or Promised Land, the new primary schools of Great Britain, above all (though not exclusively by any means) in Leicestershire County. There we saw schools, at first a small handful, later many more, doing what we knew we wanted to do, and we saw, with a surprise that surprised us—we had not been aware how deep was our own distrust of children— that these schools really worked. They were not all alike or equally good; some were inspired, some plodding, some only going through the motions of something that in their hearts they did not believe in. But, serving children of all kinds of backgrounds, operating often in old, dingy, and overcrowded buildings, working in most cases with a teacher-pupil ratio fixed by law at forty to one, and spend- ing vastly less on equipment than almost any American school, these British schools were incomparably better, by any standards including quite traditional ones, than the "best" schools we had taught in and seen in our own country.

This is a book by, and about, some of those early Ameri- can voyagers to England. It is not a description of life in British primary schools; it would take the best part of a book to describe in any detail even one day in one class- room, since it would have to be an account of how each of forty very active and involved children spent a day in a room full of interesting things to work with and other chil- dren working with them. This book is instead an attempt by some of these visitors to understand and make clear to others what is happening in these schools, what is needed to make it work, why it works, and why nothing else will work. It is as close as we have come yet, and per- haps ever will come, to a book about the theory of what has elsewhere been called student-directed learning, or non-coercive, or non-authoritarian, or more-choice-less- fear education, and what the authors call open education —perhaps the best term of all. It is not at all a book about what to do, but most parents or teachers or other school people who read and understand it will find that they can think of plenty of things to do on their own.

THE CHILD AS AN INDEPENDENT AGENT; THE TEACHER AS TRAVEL AGENT

In two chapters in the middle of the book Charles Rathbone and Roland Barth list and examine the principles and assumptions of open education. This summing up is the best I have seen. It gives a description and definition of open education that is broad enough, and yet precise enough, so that we may begin to use the phrase widely with some hope that most of those who hear it will, at least in general, know or be able to figure out what we mean. And it makes clear that open education is not so much about new ways of arranging chairs in a class, or new kinds of materials to use, as it is about new attitudes. Of the most important of these Rathbone writes:

Most essential in this psychological climate is the condition of autonomy—not only the fact of it but the child's appreciation of and belief in that fact [emphasis mine]. *Being expected to have as an independent agent and living in an environment that assumes that every child has the innate capacity and urge to make sense of the world and to make meaningful decisions concerning his own activities in that world —these expectations do have their effects on the child. They teach him to accept himself as a maker of meaning and as someone whose choices count. They teach, however obliquely, a self-respect and self-esteem— in short, a view of himself as an agent.*

It would be impossible to say more clearly and fully just what it is that most schools do not teach, do not try to teach, and in most cases try not to teach. It is a hardy and fortunate child indeed who can survive conventional schooling, however successful he may be at it, with much left of his self-respect and self-esteem—though he may have had his vanity puffed up, which is not the same

3

thing, by having been told and made to feel a thousand times and in many different ways that he is cleverer and therefore better than most people. What Rathbone is saying about these new schools is that in them, to use a small and old-fashioned word, the child is *trusted*. This is the heart of open education, what it is really all about, and it is the part most resisted and least understood. There are a great many people in the United States, and I suspect in Great Britain as well, who are willing to try, or tolerate, or even embrace the British primary style *only* because they think it will prove a more effective way to make children learn the things they have wanted them to learn all along. But this approach misses the point, and when people undertake open education in this spirit, they almost certainly fail for this reason above all others—that the children know they are not serious.

A few years ago, in one of our western states, I visited a brand-new and famous high school, built at enormous expense to house and support a program in which the students would direct their own studies, using various activity and topic centers as they saw fit. Within a year of the school's opening, the program had already been heavily cut back, and the school was moving rapidly into conventional scheduling, classes, and the like. One teacher, explaining this backsliding, said that it was because the students weren't ready to direct their own programs and just hung around talking to each other—something, by the way, they had probably rarely had a chance to do in school and perhaps needed very much. In any case, I think the teacher was probably wrong in his diagnosis. I think it far more likely that the students sensed that their teachers did not really believe in them and were not really offering them a chance to direct their own learning, but were only expecting and hoping that they would do voluntarily what formerly they had done only under the pressure of bribes and threats. This holiday from regular school can't last, the student thought, but while it is here, let's make the best of it and not waste it by doing what we're soon going to be made to do anyway. This scenario has been repeated hundreds of times in schools and classrooms that tried to adopt the forms of open education without its spirit.

Later in Rathbone's chapter, a quote from Allan Leitman gives the best statement or description I know of the open teacher's true work and function, what he has to do and does when he gives up his old jobs of straw boss, cop, and judge.

A teacher of young children is in a sense a travel agent. He helps a child go where the child wants to go. He counsels on the best way of getting there, indicating the kind of currency and the rate of exchange, the necessary "shots," the books that will help the traveler understand what he sees. He warns that some places are too dangerous or too difficult to visit just now.

I am more grateful than I can say for that metaphor, which I have also heard from my friend the psychologist Marshall Rosenberg. No metaphor seems to me to describe so fully what the helper of learning has to do and how he does it and why it works. Most analogies break down if pursued very far, but this one seems to fit even in quite small details. The travel agent induces the learner to learn, to travel into new experiences, by making the unexplored new world seem attractive and open, by finding out what kind of a trip the learner would most like to take, and by helping him take it—not, however, by taking it with him and least of all by making him prove when he comes home that he really went where he said he would go.

Early in his very important chapter, Roland Barth makes a most significant statement:

Open educators do not see adults as the unique suppliers of the elements of the external world that will release the child's potential for motivation. The world is there, and children, just by being in and of the world, have their own access to it.

The world is there. This reminds me of how many times when talking to adults about open education, I am asked, usually angrily, a question about like this, "But aren't you asking every child to reinvent the wheel?" One man not long ago asked me this in the front hall of a new high school, through whose plate glass doors we could see the school parking lot and the hundred or so cars parked in it. I said, "They don't have to invent it. It's *been* invented. It's out there. All they have to do is look to see it. Do you suppose that if we didn't tell them about the wheel, they would never notice it? And not only is the wheel out there, but so is electricity, and law, and government, and music, and everything else that makes and is made by our culture. Any child who is really *in* the world knows about them or soon will. Do you suppose that even if we tried, we could keep them a secret?"

FOSTERING SELF-CONFIDENCE

Barth then goes on to raise some points and to ask some questions that are important for several reasons. One is that they go to the heart of what open learning is about. Another is that they will surely be asked by many conventional educators. The third is that they reveal how deeply rooted in Barth, as, I suspect, in most academics today, are modes or habits of thought that make it very difficult for them to think about, or at least talk about, phenomena of life and growth. Barth writes:

A strong self-concept on the part of the child is the sine qua non *of open education; if, and only if, the child respects himself will he be able to be responsible for his own learning. Does this mean that schools are in some fundamental way responsible for fostering self-confidence?*

One might suppose from this that self-concept (or self-esteem or self-respect) was a two-valued quality. Either

6

one has it or he doesn't. Of course it is no such thing. Not only can one have more or less of it, but it is indeed a multi-dimensioned quality; one might have considerable respect for his own ability in certain areas and none at all in others. It would be more true to life to say, *"To the extent that* the child respects himself will he be able to be responsible for his own learning." It clearly follows that, yes, schools are in the most fundamental way responsible for fostering self-confidence or, rather, for making available to children situations or experiences from which they are likely to gain increased self-confidence. The distinction is important. Schools and teachers, many of them at least, have long been in the business of trying to make children feel good by telling them that they are good. It doesn't work, and not least of all because it is not convincing to tell people that you think they are bright, capable, or the like, if at the same time you treat them as if they were fools, slaves, and criminals.

As Barth continues, another complication emerges:

But what is self-esteem? What are the minimum components of self-confidence that would permit one to say a child has it? A circular argument underlies the reasoning here. If a child is capable of making important choices affecting his own learning, he has a strong self-concept; if he has a strong self-concept, he will be able to make responsible choices. Looked at in another way, children who are trusted to make choices may develop self-control; those with self-control are more likely to be trusted to make choices.

The important point here is that open educators have not yet considered, let alone established, a relationship between development of self-confidence and the ability to make responsible choices about learning. So far, the two are seen as necessary to one another, but the nature of the relationship remains to be spelled out.

Barth wants to be able to draw, or have us draw for him, a line that will enable him to say, when a child crosses it, *"Now* he has self-esteem." But there is no such line, and no way to find or make one. The relationship between self-esteem and the ability to choose is just as he describes it. But he goes on to say and, unless I misread him, to complain that the argument is circular. He then says that open educators have not considered what this relationship is. Not so. I in my books, George Dennison in *The Lives of Children,* and many others, including some of the contributors to this book, have considered it very carefully and at great length. The argument is circular for the most natural reason in the world—because the relationship itself is. The two qualities depend on each other, nurture each other, grow or decline together. Life is full of such examples. I happen to like exercise and sport. The more I exercise, the better condition I get in; the better my condition, the more I *can* exercise. Reality is not linear but circular or, better yet, spherical and multi-dimensional, with many things dependent in many ways on many other things. It is only words, and our word-dominated logic, that are linear, so that a given thing must always seem to be ahead of or behind some other given thing. Only on lists can we say that New York is *ahead* of Chicago or *behind*. Otherwise such statements are nonsense.

This point seems to me worth stressing. We are hooked, not just on linearity—what comes first?—but on causality—what causes what?—As Alan Watts says in *The Book,* we are constantly taking pieces of reality, processes of life and growth that are one, cutting or tearing them in half, and then getting into agonized or furious arguments about which of the two parts is the cause of the other. In this case, is self-esteem the cause of being able to choose, or vice versa? I agree very strongly with Watts that we must see this way of thinking not as a virtue of our culture, not even as an odd habit, but as a very serious and crippling philosophical disease of which we desperately need to cure ourselves. Nowhere is this more true than in the field of open education.

THE IMPORTANCE OF PLAY

In the second of two excerpts The Plowden Report discusses at length why play is important and useful for children, as their most natural and effective way of understanding the world around them and their own place and possibilities in it. All this is most well and truly said; it could not be improved upon. But I would like to add to it. One might feel, reading the Report, that play is fine for little children, and even the best thing for them, but that after a while they must outgrow it and learn more "serious" or "adult" ways of learning. This would be a great mistake. The fact is that in their play children are very often doing things very much like what adults do in their work. Like the economist, the traffic engineer, the social planner, or the computer expert, children at play often make models of life or certain parts of life, models they hope are a fair, if simpler, representation of the world, so that by working these models they may attain some idea of how the world works or might work or what they may do in it.

More important, what makes our truly inventive and creative thinkers, whether political, artistic, or scientific, what sets them apart from the great run of us, is, above all, that they can still play with their minds. They have not forgotten how to do it nor grown ashamed nor afraid of it. They like it, and they do it every chance they have; it is as natural to them as breathing. The ordinary, "serious," nonplayful man cannot escape things as they are; though he is always talking about "facing reality," he is as trapped by his notion of reality as any rat in a cage. For him, whatever is, is all there can be. The playful man is always saying, and cannot help saying, "But suppose things weren't this way, didn't have to be this way. Let's just for the fun of it imagine what might happen if this were different, if we did that instead of this . . ." *Just for the fun of it.* Now we know

9

from experience that out of such play may come, and often do come, ideas that may change the whole shape of human life and thought. But the playful man doesn't necessarily start with this in mind. He doesn't say to himself, like certain fanatics at their sports, "If I grind my teeth together and play hard enough, I will come up with a great idea." He plays for fun, ready to discard as useless and without regret, as he has many times in the past, most of the ideas that come to him. When a good one comes along, he is ready for it, open to it. Then a more directed thinking may begin, less like what the ordinary man calls "play," more like what he would call "work," though to the truly creative person there is no difference.

It is not hard to see why a stable society would find such men unsettling and dangerous and would try to silence or do away with them if possible. Indeed, they might be right to do so. But a society like ours, facing life-or-death crises and predicaments about which nobody knows what to do and about which most people think nothing at all can be done, needs for its very survival not just a few but hundreds of thousands, indeed a whole new generation, of people who can play.

CRITICISMS AND DANGERS, PRESENT AND FUTURE

What is the future, what are the prospects of the revolution in British primary education? The contributors to this book do not discuss this directly, but from their tone one has the feeling that the revolution is established, secure, and bound to grow. I am not so sure—for a number of reasons. It is worth noting, for example, that the rigid, anxious, tense, and pressure-ridden Meadow School described so well by Anthony Kallet had begun as a very radical and free-thinking school; even at the time of his writing, it was believed by others and honestly believed itself to be open, experimental, deeply dedicated to new ideas in education and, above all, to the life and growth of individual children. "A conservative," a friend of mine used to say, "is a man who worships a dead radical." We have seen in Montessori schools how quickly even the most creative ideas can freeze into rigid orthodoxies. The same thing could happen in British primary education.

There is another danger. In their chapters Charles Rathbone and Roland Barth state very clearly and fully the assumptions on which open education are based. It would be natural and tempting to assume that for one reason or another many or most of the parents of primary school children in Leicestershire and in other counties having open schools more or less understand what these assumptions are and accept them. I think this is very far from the truth. Primary schools in England have been able to make changes on a wide scale largely for two reasons. In the first place, there is a tradition that schools and teachers know best, that what they do is none of the parents' business, and that parents should not stick their noses in school affairs. Thus in most communities, certainly until very recently, a suggestion to form an organization like an American PTA would probably be viewed as wildly radical and rejected with horror by teachers and parents alike. Secondly, and much more important, the parents of almost all these children do not expect in the slightest that their children will later go on to a university but rather that they will leave school at fifteen or sixteen and take their places somewhere in the working or lower middle class. Most parents who expect and want their children to go to a university do not, if they can help it, send their children to government primary schools at all. In short, most British parents have not seen or felt their society as being very upwardly mobile, or felt it their chief duty in life to shove their children up the socio-economic ladder, or seen school and success in school as a way to do this.

Though I do not know, I suspect this attitude is changing, and as it changes, as adults tend more and more to see school as a place where children start a race that will go on all the rest of their lives, the primary school revolution may be deeply threatened. Indeed it is already threatened by members of a self-styled elite who want to keep Britain a rigid and hierarchical society. These enemies of open education see much more clearly than most of its supporters the long-run political and social consequences of this kind of schooling. To a man, my teacher friends in new British primary schools do not think that the ground they have gained can be lost. I hope they are right, but I fear they may be overconfident.

There is a kind of hidden assumption, unstated, perhaps unconscious and unintentional, that when we talk about open education, we are talking about the education of young children. The contributors to this book have themselves done almost all their work, at least their work in open education, with young children. The schools they have visited and worked with in England, which they describe and from which they draw their examples and their conclusions, are all primary schools, most of them infant schools (ages five to seven). Of the books and pamphlets listed in the bibliography, almost all are about primary education; only one of the British publications is about secondary education at all, and from its description (I have not seen it), it is more about what ought to happen than what is happening. In my visits to Leicestershire County and in many discussions, there and here with primary school teachers and heads, I have never heard of any movement to carry into secondary education the kinds of reforms they have carried out in their own schools or, indeed, any thinking or discussion about what reformed secondary education might be like. On the whole I think it is fair to say, first, that in Great Britain very little is being done in, or even written about, open secondary education, and that in any case the contributors to this book have not so far been greatly interested in it.

This, if true, seems to me a mistake and a quite serious

one. There is irony here. The contributors to this book would, I feel sure, consider themselves in no way supporters of A. S. Neill or Summerhill, more probably as severe critics or even opponents. Yet in what seems to me a vital respect, the British primary schools described and discussed here, and their counterparts in the States, are very like Summerhill. They are, though in rather different ways, islands, monasteries, would-be paradises for children. The best of them *are* wonderful places, no doubt about it. But they are, with very few exceptions, cut off from the world and from the problems and crises of our societies and times. They avoid the question of how a young person may best grow up in these times and deal with these problems, even the problem of their next and very different school. Both Summerhill and the British primary schools act, on the whole, as if the outside world was not there or was there only as a kind of Given, that nothing much could be done about. Let me put this a bit differently. These schools, while the child is in them, do indeed treat him as an agent and give him a great deal of the direction of his own life and growth. But they do not take much time to consider, or help him consider, how or where he may be able to continue to act like an agent once he has left. They seem to say, in effect, "Within these walls you can be the director of your life, free, responsible, making choices, and acting on them. After you leave here, that is all over, and you will have to live like other people, doing what you are told, taking what comes to you." Thus, these schools are less a part of the whole of his life than an interlude away from it—a breathing spell, or as another British open educator (Lyward) once put it, "a respite."

I have no intrinsic objection to this. In fact, to people who say that if you can't reform the whole school system, there is no use in reforming a part of it, I have always said that even in terms of preparing a child for a life that may be difficult and dull, one good year in school is better

13

than none. I only wonder whether an educational revolution as profound as open education can survive in the long run unless it is or becomes a part of a wider and deeper notion or vision of life and of social change. Without some such connection, some such vision, I fear that it may either lose its vitality and capacity for growth or that it may be isolated and destroyed by those who see more clearly to what social and political consequences it might someday lead.

TWO CLASSROOMS

by Anthony Kallet

I want to describe two classrooms in which I have worked during the past few years: one is in England, one in the United States. In what follows I am relying on memory abetted by some notes and, while I realize the impossibility of attaining objectivity, I shall try to keep closely to factual statements unless I clearly label what I am saying as opinion. The names of the schools and teachers are fictitious.

FIRST GRADE AT THE MEADOW SCHOOL, U.S.A.

During the fall and winter of 1962 I spent about four months as an apprentice teacher in Miss Jones' first-grade class at the Meadow School. Miss Jones was an experienced teacher who had been at Meadow for many years. There were twenty-one children in her class and, besides Miss Jones and me, there was a part-time assistant.

The children, almost all of whom had been in the school since they were four, came primarily from upper middle-class homes. Their fathers were university professors, lawyers, doctors, and businessmen. The school was a private one, and tuition was fairly high, although there were one or two children in the class on scholarship. With a single exception, the children were near their sixth birthday at the beginning of the year. One boy of seven was repeating the first grade for academic reasons.

15

Two first-grade classes shared a building. In addition to her classroom, in Miss Jones' half of the building there was a workshop, through a door at the rear. The main classroom was about twenty by thirty feet (if memory serves me), with windows along one wall and two doors leading to the outside, the main entrance at the rear and a door at the side opening onto the playground. The desks, each labelled with a child's name, were arranged in a sort of horseshoe, a column down each side of the room and two rows at the rear. There was some open space behind the last row, including a small alcove containing a piano, bookshelf, cupboard, and table. Along the wall opposite the windows were open lockers and cubbies for the children's coats and personal belongings. Two children shared each locker and cubby. At the front of the room was a blackboard and, in the open end of the horseshoe, there was a table that might be used in teaching. The teacher's desk was in a front corner and was not much used except for storage. Another desk at the back was shared by the assistant and me. Along the wall under the windows were tables and shelves for plants, some building blocks, and various science materials—leaves, shells, and so forth.

The first-graders at Meadow did not stay all day. School began at eight-forty and ended at noon. During the second term half the class stayed one afternoon a week in alternate weeks. The morning was divided into several periods, each lasting between fifteen or twenty minutes and half an hour. The last period might be somewhat longer, perhaps forty or forty-five minutes. The best way to give an impression of the class in action might be to describe a composite day.

The children, who might have arrived at school from eight o'clock on, were called to their desks when it was time to begin, and attendance was taken, after which a child was sent with the slip to the main office. On Monday Miss Jones or I would ask for volunteers for a number of jobs to be done during the week, including watering the plants, taking the attendance slip to the office, being line leader (to head up the line when children moved from the classroom to another part of the school), and so forth. Morning "chores" were usually followed by a few minutes during which children could come to the front of the room and share with the class any news they might have or show items of interest they had brought with them.

At nine o'clock the science specialist might come in for half an hour of science, often bringing a variety of things with her; I remember particularly a live iguana, and there was always her dog. On another day the children would go to the music room for half an hour of singing and dancing. The first period on still another day might be devoted to "central subject" which, in this class, was pre-historic man. Once a week the school day began with an assembly in the main hall.

At about nine-thirty it might be time for mathematics. Each child had a bag of Cuisenaire rods hung on his own hook at the front of the room (where his reader was also stored), and the children might be asked to get these and take them to their desks. Sometimes they were allowed a few minutes of free play with the rods, and then Miss Jones would demonstrate a type of problem or perhaps call a few children to the front of the room to try it. Activities with the rods were fairly closely supervised by the teacher, and specific tasks were set. On other occasions the children would do problems on worksheets that had been prepared and duplicated by Miss Jones. She would again demonstrate, or have several children demonstrate, the kind of problem to be done, and there might be discussion of the principles involved. When the children had finished a paper, they would take it to the back of the room and place it in a tray on my desk to be corrected and, if there were mistakes, handed back the next day for revision. Sometimes there was a selection of papers available, and children could work through as many as they wished. During the mathematics period, as during the writing period that followed, the two or three adults would move around the room answering questions. Children were not, in general, permitted to move around the room or talk with one another during work periods, although they were free to go to the toilet. It was expected that during "academic" periods, except when there was class discussion, the only conversation would be between a child and a teacher.

Twenty minutes of mathematics might be followed, sometimes after a break of two or three minutes during which children could stretch and walk around and talk, by a writing period. During most of the first term this was largely devoted to presenting a new letter (children would be called to the board to practice making it) and playing various games involving the new sound. The children would then be given papers on which the letter had been formed, and they would trace and copy it.

A reading period might follow at about nine-fifty or ten o'clock. Soon after the term began, the children were divided into three reading groups, according to Miss Jones' estimation of their ability. During the term children might be moved from one group to another. Each group would go with a teacher to a different part of the room: one group went into the workshop. The reader was of the Dick-and-Jane type, and the procedure was for each child in turn to read a few lines aloud. Flash cards with words from the readers were often used, and various reading games might be played from time to time, but the main activity was reading aloud from the books. (I found it exceptionally difficult to maintain discipline, especially when I was working with the "slowest" group. Occasionally it would be necessary to ask a child to remain behind after the reading period, which meant that he would miss part of recess.) Later in the term, when many children had gained some proficiency in reading, this round robin reading period was supplemented by another that was somewhat freer. The children would choose a book from a selection at the back of the room, and their choice would be approved and recorded by the teacher. As children read, the teachers would again circulate, listening to them read, helping them select new books, and so forth. Children who had finished a particular book might sometimes listen to other children read from it. At the beginning of the second term, these reading and writing periods were further supplemented by a period (during the afternoon session in alternate weeks) when children were introduced to composition. They might be given a sentence to start them off, or the teacher might suggest a theme or a question.

After reading, at about ten-twenty or ten-thirty, was recess time, and the children would go to the playground where they would find the other first-grade class and the second-graders. They could use a slide, swings, climbing apparatus, a ball, large wooden blocks for building, and so on. Most of the teachers of the four classes were on the playground during recess; there might be sixty or eighty children and four or five adults present.

Recess, which generally lasted fifteen or twenty minutes, was followed by milk and crackers, which had been set out by one of the teachers. Following this mid-morning snack, at about eleven o'clock, was a rest period. Each child would pick a mat from a storage fixture at the back of the room and lie down; one of the teachers would read to the class. (Again, I found this a situation in which it was difficult, at times, to maintain discipline. Children wanted to talk or move their mats together, and this was frowned upon unless it could be done without too much disturbance. I often had to stop reading to speak to children who were disturbing the class.)

After rest a child would be appointed "mat caller" and would call the other children, one at a time, to put their mats away. The last period of the morning might be devoted to art (once a week) or music in the classroom with the music teacher (also once a week), to some reading

19

aloud, or to work on one of the subjects that had not been touched upon earlier. I recall that mathematics was sometimes done at this time, but never reading or writing.

At the end of the morning the children would put on their coats and line up at the back of the room. When the line was quiet, the class would move off, the line leader and a teacher at the head of it, to the main building where the children would be met by their parents. I should note that children were not permitted to talk when in line moving from one place to another, although at times this rule was not too strictly enforced.

I want now to summarize my impressions of Miss Jones' class. It was, generally speaking, a fairly tightly controlled situation. The individual child had few decisions to make at any point. The daily schedule was posted next to the blackboard in front of the room, showing the order of activities for the day, and children knew, or should have known, what was expected of them. There was time during the day for discussion, but almost never was this child-to-child discussion; it was discussion with the teacher as the focus and children talking to her. The degree of tightness of control can be illustrated by my recollection that once, after giving a mathematics lesson, I was criticized by Miss Jones for having allowed two children in the back row to slide their desks together. In my recollection discipline problems loom large. There were one or two children who were distinct "problems," and often I felt that there was an undercurrent of things about to get out of hand. Miss Jones was so experienced that the situation rarely flew apart when she was in charge of the class, but even she had to work quite hard to keep the lid on what so often seemed to be a pot about to boil.

Symptomatic of the tightness of control was the rule about not talking when in line; indeed, the concept of moving children around in a line in itself indicates a fair degree of control being imposed. In the first grade at the Meadow School, and as far as I could tell throughout the whole school, decisions typically were made by adults for children. In the first grade this meant that reading groups were determined by the teacher, the seating arrangement was determined by the teacher, and the order of activities during the day and the amount of time spent on each were determined by the teacher. Within a given lesson, children had little say about what they did; they were presented with a task and they carried it out. In writing, the letter-of-the-day was already on their paper. In reading, the teacher assigned the lines each child was to read.

The freest periods during the week were the music periods, but here again the problems of discipline, of simply keeping the noise down to a manageable level, were often so great that the exceptionally gifted woman who taught music seemed at times almost defeated by the task of keeping these twenty-odd children in order. Control was again indicated by the need (and it was a real need—or should I say it *became* a real need because it was assumed to be a real need) to have several teachers on duty on the playground during recess. Control again was in the fore when, on that single day in alternate weeks during the second term, half of the children stayed for lunch, and a teacher was assigned to each table of five. (The pattern of one or two teachers to six or eight children at meals prevailed throughout the school.)

Some children appeared to manage quite well despite all this control, but for others, especially the "problem" children, I often felt that the control was too much, that they were being held too tightly in check, that too little was permitted them in the way of free behavior, that their problems were, in part, being created rather than mitigated by control. No, this is not quite an accurate statement: I said "I often felt," whereas, in fact, I can see this now in retrospect; when I was in the classroom, it did truly seem that every single control imposed was necessary if anything was to be accomplished.

AN INFANT CLASS AT HILLSIDE COUNTY
PRIMARY SCHOOL, ENGLAND

During the autumn term of 1963 I spent several hours a week observing, and working informally with children in Miss Smith's class at Hillside. I was in no sense an official teacher of the class at any time, and so my experience with the class was not only less extensive than my experience with the first grade at Meadow but also different in kind. In both situations, however, I was able to do a lot of looking and listening.

Miss Smith was a first-year teacher, just out of the Froebel Educational Institute in London; this was her first class. The children in the class, one of three parallel infant classes in the school, came from families living in the school district, a prosperous suburb in the Midlands of England. Like the children at Meadow, most of these children came from middle-class homes, although many more of their fathers were in business than in the professions. There were, among the fathers, a good number of artisans, highly skilled, well-paid workers in the light industries of the neighboring city. The children in the class ranged in age, at the beginning of the year, from four years ten months to six years nine months. That is, it was a vertically grouped class comprising children of all the ages covered by the term "infant." For the youngest children this was their first term in school; the oldest might have been in school four or five terms. Because of the intake of new five-year-olds three times a year, and because children move into the junior school only once a year, the class grew from about thirty children in September to about forty in April. During the period I was with the class, it numbered about thirty, perhaps one or two more.

The room, about the same size as the first-grade classroom at Meadow but without the workshop space, was attractive but crowded. On the far side were windows and a French door leading to the grassy playing field. The main entrance lead off a corridor, which was also used as a makeshift activity area; part of the corridor was enclosed and part open on one side. In the building were the other two infant classes and a junior class, the headmaster's office, a small library, and the girls' and boys' lavatories, the latter also housing the woodworking bench and tools.

There were no desks in the classroom but rather four or five groups of trapezoidal tables in pairs or in threes. Each group was associated not with specific children but with activities. Some of the tables were mainly for writing, others for number work, still others for arts and crafts, and so forth. In the back of the room next to the corridor was a Wendy (play) house equipped with toy furniture, dolls, tableware, and so forth. Next to this was a table often used by the teacher and a storage table on which the children's writing books were kept. Under the windows were tables for number apparatus, a sand table, and a water table. Along the front wall was the library, partially screened from the rest of the room by a divider; the books were in racks on the wall, and there were several chairs turned to face the wall. Next to the library were two double painting easels. Interspersed among all these pieces of equipment were several storage units. A table along the corridor wall was used part of the morning for a milk bar.

The school day at Hillside began at nine o'clock and continued until three-forty-five, with a meal break from noon until one-thirty. The day usually began with a short religious service (required by law), which was held in one of the three infant rooms. Following this the children returned to their own classroom, and Miss Smith marked the register and took the names of the children staying for lunch. She then went through a list of the various activities available in the room and asked children to raise their hands for the one they wanted to start the day with; for each activity there was a maximum permissible number of children. Among the choices would be painting, building with blocks, reading, writing, woodwork, sand and water play, Wendy house, clay or model-making, and any special activities Miss Smith might have set up. When all the children had chosen, they went off and started to work.

Their choices were only starting points in some cases, and during the course of the morning children might move from one part of the room to another as they finished what they were doing. Conversely, a child might choose to spend the entire morning, or even the whole day, working at a single project. As space became available in one place (for example, a child might leave the Wendy house), and other children could move in. Aside from the initial choice, the process of selecting an activity was informal. Miss Smith might, on occasion, ask a particular child or a small group to do something she had in mind, but the children were largely left to make their own choices, within the limitations of space and equipment. The afternoon was organized in much the same way, and at the end of the day Miss Smith would call the class together for a period of discussion, or she might read aloud to them.

Considering the number of things going on and the number of children in the room, the atmosphere in Miss Smith's class was generally calm and collected. (I should point out that seldom were all the children in the room at the same time. There would be one or two in the corridor, one or two in the library around the corner, where more "advanced" books were kept and which was open to both infants and juniors, and one or two at the woodworking bench in the boys' lavatory.) Most of the children in the classroom would be moving about, talking quietly, and doing a good job of keeping out of each other's way; only rarely did Miss Smith have to request that the noise level be kept down. The sheer density of children and apparatus meant that now and again a tower of blocks would come crashing down or someone's paints would be upset or water would slosh onto the floor, but this caused little confusion; the child involved picked up the pieces or mopped up and went on working.

In this classroom, reading, writing, and mathematics were not treated as separate "subjects," and it took me quite a while to discover just how, for example, a child learned to read. An important element, I am sure, was that reading was "in the air." There were always older children reading and writing, and I often saw a little one sitting near a big one trying to imitate his activity. Upon entering the class in his first term, each child was given a large, unlined "free writing book" with his name on the cover. He was free to do what he liked in this book. Part of the "free" in "free writing" stemmed from the child's growing awareness that what he put in this book was his own and would not be corrected by the teacher—save in cases of complete incomprehensibility. At first most children drew pictures with pencil or crayon. Now and then Miss Smith might discuss what the child was doing with his book and perhaps write a sentence or two in it, which the child was to trace or copy. Soon he would be given a small notebook to serve as his personal dictionary, to supplement word cards on the wall and a homemade class dictionary. He might, when he asked for a word, be requested to guess what the first sound was, or later Miss Smith would ask him what letter he thought the word began with. Phonetic skills were developed, but the process was informal. (There was, however, nothing informal about the detailed records Miss Smith kept of representative examples of each child's work throughout the year.)

There was, as I have said, a library corner and a library room nearby. The younger children, perhaps at first mainly because they saw older ones doing it, would go over and take a book to look at. Miss Smith would come by now and then and read with someone or listen to someone read. There seemed to be little anxiety about reading. Children were encouraged to read and to write as they wished, and a considerable number of them wished to often. Books the children wrote would be prominently displayed and read by other children, which may also have been an important source of motivation. Perhaps in part as a result of the low anxiety level Miss Smith appeared to have about reading and writing, there seemed to me to be only one or two of the older children who were not reading at a level one might deem appropriate for their age, and the mass of free writing these fives and sixes and sevens turned out was astonishing.

There was little formal number work in this infant class although, since the room was full of material with mathematical potential, much of which was attractive, a fair number of children were using some sort of number-related equipment almost all the time. Among the available apparatus were Cuisenaire rods, Dienes' multi-base blocks, geometric sorting sets, attribute blocks, counting apparatus including beads and abaci, scales, liquid measures, and so forth.

Painting, model-making, clay, collage, paper cutting and folding, all these were, it seemed to me, accorded as high a status in the scheme of things as reading and writing and mathematics; I felt that the amount of time Miss Smith spent on the arts in the course of a morning was about equal to that she spent on "the Rs." There was invariably a quartet of children at the easels, someone working with clay, someone else out at the woodworking bench. The Wendy house was in continuous use—was, indeed, perhaps the most popular single activity for the younger children and some of the older ones. An adjunct to play in the Wendy house was a fine collection of dress-up clothes, and it was not at all unusual for a child, boy or girl, to put on an outlandish costume and traipse around the room, or down the corridor, to show it to his or her friends. There always seemed to be laughter and high spirits in the Wendy corner, which at times infected much of the rest of the room to good advantage.

In the midst of all of this Miss Smith might one moment be discussing a model rocket with two or three boys and the next be listening to a seven-year-old read, or perhaps she would simply stand for a minute or two and watch a child building a tower with some blocks, asking a question, making a comment or not as the situation seemed to warrant. She never seemed rushed or harried, and her calm most often communicated itself to the children, whose general enthusiasm and high spirits seldom got away from them. The range of matters to which Miss Smith attended in the course of a day was as varied as the number of things going on in the room and yet, with all this, she was able to keep fairly well in mind, I felt, the general direction of each child's activities not, perhaps, minute by minute or even day by day but certainly over a longer and possibly more meaningful span of time. Her training in observation and recording of specifics seemed to stand her in very good stead, indeed, in this complex situation.

An important element in Miss Smith's approach to teaching seemed to me that she did not readily label children as "problems." She seemed aware that thinking in terms of "problems" often helped create them, and she was willing and able to accept a fairly wide range of behavior and achievements as falling within a "normal" range.

THE TWO CLASSROOMS CONTRASTED

The contrast between Miss Jones' class and Miss Smith's could not be greater, although I certainly do not mean to imply that nothing good happened in the former and nothing untoward ever happened in the latter. In Miss Jones' class most decisions were made for the children by an adult; in Miss Smith's class each child had continually to decide for himself what he was going to do and, once having decided, he had to implement his choice, being given a lot of room to do things right— or "wrong."

In Miss Jones' class there was, I felt, a subtle but powerful undercurrent of competitiveness. For example, the reading groups, which were based upon the teacher's judgment of each child's ability, gave children a chance to demonstrate a quick intolerance of those who did not read so fluently or who needed help with a new word. In Miss Smith's classroom the proliferation of activities and equipment often meant that no two children would be working at the same task, thus making competition difficult (although probably not impossible for some children from middle-class homes). When several children were doing the same thing, like as not they would be working together. Vertical grouping made cooperation easy and natural, as older children would, quite spontaneously it seemed, pitch in and help younger ones in countless ways from spelling a word to tying an apron.

A most striking difference between the two learning situations was in the self-reliance of the children. It often seemed that in Miss Jones' class, and in Meadow School in general, children were deliberately protected from the need to rely on themselves. For example, on painting day, Thursday of each week, Miss Jones and I would spend twenty minutes or so before school pouring the paint into muffin tins, a tin for each child. We would put each child's name on a piece of paper and, when painting time came around at the end of the morning, we would hand out the paper and the paints. We did most of the washing up afterwards. (Indeed, and I blush to admit that at the time I saw nothing wrong with it, in this classroom we even sharpened the children's pencils once a week.)

In Miss Smith's class a child who had decided to paint

took out the canisters of paint, poured out the powder, added water, got a brush, painted, put away the paint, and cleaned up his tins. Naturally, there was help available for the younger ones who needed it—either help by Miss Smith or, more often, by one of the older children. By the time they were six, almost all these children had mastered a wide variety of housekeeping skills without the exercise of which the situation simply would not have been viable.

The general assumption in Miss Jones' class, unspoken of course, was that adults knew best and children took and did what was given to them. In Miss Smith's class children quickly came to realize that they were expected to seek out and cope with self-chosen aspects of a richly complex environment and that the teacher and other children would help when necessary—but not take over the job and hence preclude learning.

There is little question in my mind that in many aspects of their work the children in Miss Smith's class were achieving results that surpassed those of the children at Meadow. Most of the six-year-olds who had been in school two or three terms were writing copiously and often quite creatively, almost always illustrating what they wrote —or writing about what they drew. They wrote stories, poems, even little plays. Indeed, I would judge that the writing of many of these children surpassed in both quantity and quality that being done by the children two years older at Meadow. An important reason, of course, was that they were writing when they chose and about subjects they chose and that they were writing for other children, not just the teacher, to read.

It is harder to compare the mathematics work since nothing formal was done in Hillside until the children reached the junior part of the school. Certainly Miss Smith's children were having a variety of experiences with mathematical materials of all sorts under conditions that made discovery possible. The art seemed to me at least as creative at Hillside as at Meadow, and there was, of course, vastly more of it since so much more time was devoted to it and it was so highly valued as an activity.

Here, then, are two classrooms as they were some time ago. I imagine that neither Miss Jones nor Miss Smith is teaching now just as she was teaching then, but based upon my experience in the two rooms as I have tried to portray them, I have little doubt which provided more suitable conditions for children to explore and grow, which provided children with more scope for important learning, which manifested in everything that went on a greater respect for and acceptance of the uniqueness of each child.

LEICESTERSHIRE REVISITED

by William P. Hull

This is an account of Mr. Hull's visit, with David Armington, to the schools of Leicestershire County during the spring of 1964. It is, in his words, "an attempt to sort out my own reactions and impressions in a way which may be useful in understanding some of the educational problems we face in this country."

A number of times during my visit to Leicestershire County in England I found myself wishing that I could share certain scenes with others. A brief glimpse of some rather ordinary kinds of activities might do more to convince people of the significance of what has been happening in the County than any description or commentary. In this report I will both describe and comment, while continuing to wish that it were possible for readers to see for themselves some of the things I will talk about.

Visiting schools in the County, one soon becomes accustomed to the patterns of organization that allow children much greater freedom and responsibility than is traditionally granted them elsewhere. One quickly comes to assume that primary education everywhere would have evolved along similar lines were it not crippled by false values and assumptions. What seems to have been achieved in some of these schools is the logical extension and development of ideas tried in the United States by a few schools during the era of progressive education.

Some of us who have visited there believe that the best of the Leicestershire County schools represent a stage of educational development well in advance of what has been reached in the States. We are left, however, with a number of puzzling questions:

Why is it, for example, that these things could be achieved in at least one county in England but not in public schools in the United States? Why is it that many or most other English school systems have not been developing in the same direction? (There are indications that healthy changes may be occurring elsewhere in England, though perhaps not on so wide a scale as in Leicestershire. I have no first-hand knowledge of developments elsewhere.) What problems would one encounter in attempting to achieve some of the same reforms in American schools? What would be the chances of success in such an undertaking? It may well be that a major problem in the United States is that schools that once had progressive tendencies have moved slowly away from some of their original healthy practices without realizing the kinds of pressures that have caused the drift. What have these pressures been? Why have their effects so often been insidious and virtually ignored?

It is not easy to analyze a complexity compounded of differences in culture, values, and traditions. What appears on the surface to be the result of a natural process of evolution may involve factors that have yet to be isolated or described in ways that make their significance apparent. To create a Leicestershire-type learning environment in the States might prove considerably more difficult than some people seem to think when they come away from the County. While I am encouraged by such optimism on the part of so many, I fear that the task may require a good deal more insight and practical know-how than the too-often backward profession of education has shown for some years.

CHARACTERISTICS OF INFANT SCHOOLS

One of the startling experiences Dave Armington and I had shortly after our arrival in Leicestershire was to watch children coming to morning assembly in an infant school. More than four hundred five-, six-, and seven-year-olds walked into the main auditorium from their classrooms, alone or in small groups, found places for themselves on the floor, and sat talking with each other during the ten minutes before the start of the short religious service. The children did not come into the hall in lines accompanied by teachers; they did not sit according to classes or any other prearranged plan. The teachers arrived after most of the children and sat on chairs around the outside of the group. Occasionally, during the waiting period, children would move from one place to another. The noise level was low. There did not seem to be a single word from any of the teachers for the purpose of restraining or controlling the children; there was no need for such measures. The scene reminded me of an adult audience waiting for the beginning of a concert. When it was time for the assembly to begin, the children, well aware that something was about to happen, stopped talking, though we could not detect the signal to which they were responding—perhaps it was merely that everyone had now arrived. I had never before seen a community of young children behaving with such freedom and self-restraint. They demonstrated an awareness about the group and a sensitivity to it, together with an ability to control their own behavior. I have never come across this combination of characteristics in a comparable group of American children.

We saw many instances of these qualities in this and in other infant schools in the County. Some of the new schools have unusual architectural designs, classrooms being grouped around a large hall that is in continuous formal and informal use by children throughout the day. We saw halls, and nearby corridors and foyers, being used for block building, reading, writing, play shopkeeping, science explorations, baking, gymnastics, and music. Classes in these schools, as in infant and junior schools throughout England and Wales, average forty children and more. One result of the large size of the classes is that teachers are not generally available to supervise activities outside their classrooms, although in larger schools the head, or the deputy head, may spend part of her time working with individual children or small groups in the hall or library. Music and gymnastics are sometimes conducted as formal classes, but throughout much of the day children may be using musical instruments and gym equipment freely on their own.

In some schools children mingle freely with each other outside of the classroom, without respect to age. The assumption that children must spend most of the day in a self-contained classroom with other children their age has been fading in the best of these infant schools, with the result that children have a sense of belonging to a much larger community than that of the individual class. In a few infant schools we visited, children are not assigned to age-groups at all. Rather than forming separate groups of fives, sixes, and sevens, these schools have vertical or "family" groups encompassing the entire infant age range from five to seven-and-a-half. There is a vibrant quality, reflecting deep involvement in what is going on and contributing to a largeness of spirit in the schools we visited.

Many infants stay at school for lunch. At some infant schools the older children, seven-year-olds, help with the lunch routines, setting up and putting away chairs and laying out silverware. On occasion there will be too few teachers for all the tables, and the older children may help to serve the younger ones. The kitchen staff will also help around the hall. It is interesting to note that in these schools, and others at both the infant and junior levels, the kitchen staff is not isolated. Often the women will be ✓ sought out by children for help with spelling words and other academic problems. Practices such as this seem to have evolved naturally out of an atmosphere in which adults and children alike are accepted in their own right and valued as members of a meaningful community.

DIFFERENCES BETWEEN LEICESTERSHIRE AND AMERICAN SCHOOLS

Our visits to the infant schools came as quite a shock to Dave and me because of the sharp contrast between what we saw there and the daily life in the schools with which we are familiar. We are accustomed to classes of twenty children with one teacher and, usually, an assistant teacher or teacher-in-training. A school assembly, which takes place once a week, requires all hands to march the children in line and to keep them from talking. Children sit by classes within reach of their teachers who are generally busy controlling disruptive behavior. Five-year-olds are considered too young to stay for lunch. Six-year-olds are introduced gradually to the heady experience of sharing a meal with their classmates, after four months of the school year have passed, by staying for lunch once a week under conditions that permit a ratio of one teacher to three children at the table. Seven-year-olds are allowed to stay for lunch three days a week and require the same teacher-pupil ratio. The responsibility of helping with lunchroom routines is a privilege reserved for fourteen-year-olds.

These are gross comparisons, easy to make because the contrast is so sharp. The contrast is emphasized further when it is kept in mind that the infants we saw in Leicestershire were in schools serving all the children in the neigh-

35

borhood, schools located next to council housing estates, the residents of the houses having been recently moved out from the slums of the inner city. The children we are most familiar with in the United States come from middle- and upper-middle-class families. The comparisons are shocking indeed for Americans and help point out the sickness that has been growing in our ambitious, prestige-oriented schools.

It is more difficult to compare the learning that takes place in the two kinds of school situations because the styles are so different. Here again, however, it is hard to avoid feeling that many American schools fare badly by comparison. We found in the best of the Leicestershire schools, both infant and junior, an involvement in their work on the part of the children, an integrity in their approach to what they were doing, that is not apparent in any American schools with which we are familiar. In the few spheres where direct comparisons are justifiable, such as work in multi-base arithmetic and in free writing, many of the Leicestershire schools were clearly ahead in terms of the calibre of the work being done. Our feeling, shared by a number of people who have visited the County, is that the climate in the best schools is much more favorable for learning than in schools in the States.

Why is it that the primary schools in Leicestershire have moved forward while so many American schools, including most of those which once pioneered in progressive education, have been going in quite a different direction? Part of the answer seems to lie in the widespread revolution in the teaching of infants, a revolution now old enough to have established traditions in many parts of England. The infant schools have shared, as have many schools in the United States, in the enlightenment that has come from studies of child development. They have been highly successful in establishing more humane and effective forms of education. The organization of the

36

schools and the age-span encompassed under the term "infant" are probably important factors. Children are admitted three times a year, near their fifth birthday, but move on into junior schools only once a year, in September, near the age of seven-and-a-half. All children, thus, have at least two years of infant education and many have three years. They are exposed over a considerable period of time to a unified pattern of teaching—in some instances they may have the same teacher for all, or most of their infant school lives. In the United States, of course, children will normally have but one year of kindergarten before first grade intervenes, usually with quite a different set of values and expectations.

The differences between the infant schools and our kindergartens extend beyond matters of organization and age-spread. In the best infant schools children learn to read, write, and work with numbers when they are ready. They are not held back and protected from such activities as they so often are in our kindergartens, nor are they coerced, face forward in formal classes, as they are in our first grades. Such flexibility is successful beyond question, whether one judges by the spirit and involvement of the children or by their ability and readiness in dealing with written English or systematic mathematics. In the best infant classes most children learn to read because reading and writing are part of the atmosphere in the room. If they do not learn readily, however, they are not fussed over or worried about. The result is that Leicestershire junior schools have few reading problems. We felt, nevertheless, that the technology of some of the work with language could be improved. There was, for example, little opportunity for the children to develop skills in phonetic analysis. But whatever the shortcomings, they are clearly offset by a philosophy and setting that encourages children to learn and gives them the freedom to do so in their own style, at their own pace.

The infant schools have a valuable heritage that has been growing for a number of years, a heritage including a wide range of interesting activities and materials as well as a spirit-giving vitality to what goes on. Such conditions do not come about automatically, but they do seem to be the natural outcome of regarding children as individuals capable of taking an active part in their own learning, instead of as disruptive creatures who need to be managed and guided through a series of detailed tasks. We know of a few outstanding nursery and kindergarten classes in the United States that are successful largely because of sensitive and skillful teachers, but these teachers must work in opposition to the philosophy prevailing in the grades above them. It was quite significant, we felt, that in Leicestershire the pattern that has proved so successful with infants has been extended beyond the classrooms of those few, rare teachers who would probably manage to teach well in any framework. It appears that when the educational climate is favorable and a good model is available, teachers who are not themselves especially gifted may be able to run a good program.

The obvious excellence of the best infant schools we saw could be very discouraging for Americans. The achievement of these schools is so far ahead of what has been happening in the States that it might seem impossibly difficult to achieve comparable results in this country in the near future. I was really quite reassured to find that not all the schools in Leicestershire have made the progress the best have made, that there are at least some County schools where education is still a grim, highly disciplined, tightly controlled undertaking. To me this meant that it may be possible for American schools to move toward more enlightened forms of education, that there are not special, mysterious forces at work that make such improvements possible in Leicestershire, but not elsewhere. Variation within the County seems considerable; some of their schools are apparently as poor as any of ours, so there may be hope here! People in the County are quite realistic about what remains to be done and have no illusions that it will be done overnight. Vivian Gibbon, until recently an advisor to infant schools, estimated that it might take six or eight years to double the number of schools doing what is currently considered the best job possible. When one recalls that there are about two hundred and fifty primary (infant and junior) schools in the County, with a student population of about 40,000, one can appreciate the magnitude of the undertaking.

Many people have been surprised at the story we have told about what is happening in Leicestershire, for such progress is apparently not typical of England in general. I can only speculate about the reasons why changes are taking place in Leicestershire. I suspect that we are seeing the results of the influence of a small group of people, the County director of education and the advisors for junior and infant schools particularly, but also a number of heads of schools and individual teachers, a group that has worked together informally as well as formally in an atmosphere relatively unaffected by parental concerns and pressures as known in American middle-class schools.

The lack of involvement of parents in schools seems to be true in England generally, although this pattern is changing slowly. What happens as a result is that changes can be made that do not necessarily accord with over-all public sentiment. Obviously changes can be good or bad, and the lack of contact between parents and school could result in the implementation of poor educational policies. In Leicestershire, however, unusually enlightened and able administrators and advisors were ready and able to encourage the best of what was being accomplished and to introduce far-reaching innovations. The influence of these people appears to have been a major factor leading toward educational reform in County schools.

39

THE LEICESTERSHIRE EXPERIMENT

Leicestershire is better known in England for the Leicestershire Experiment than for the excellence of its primary schools. The Experiment, which has been successful enough now to be called the Leicestershire Plan, consists of the gradual abolition of the eleven-plus selection examination used to determine whether a child would go to a high status grammar school or a relatively lower status secondary modern school at the end of his junior school years. The director of education and others recognized that there were serious limitations and inequities in this scheme, both for the children who passed the examination and were selected for the grammar schools and for those who were not so selected. They took seriously the fact that IQ is no longer considered by many reputable psychologists an adequate measure of intellectual functioning. They also noted the evidence from their own schools that indicated that the eleven-plus examination did a rather poor job of selecting children who could benefit from a straight "academic" education.

There were other factors, too. The examination was unpopular with many of the parents of the seventy-five percent of children who did not qualify for places in the grammar schools. In the eyes of many segments of society, and too often in their own eyes as well, these children were labeled failures at the age of eleven and a half. There was also general recognition among the people I talked with of the grave shortcomings of traditional grammar school education, though I do not know how widespread such a point of view is. Finally, parental dissatisfaction worked the other way too. Many parents of children in the grammar schools wanted art, music, and crafts available for their children.

The director and his colleagues decided, for all these reasons, that the time had come to abolish the eleven-plus examination. It was to be replaced by a two-tier secondary program in which all children at eleven and a half would go into comprehensive high schools and in which those children whose parents agreed to undertake to keep them in school for at least two more years (that is, for one year beyond the legal school-leaving age of fifteen) would go into a grammar school, the same in name as its ancestor but quite different in form and function. The use of the labels "high school" and "grammar school" is therefore different in Leicestershire than it is in the rest of England. The Leicestershire Plan is still being implemented. It entails a lot of new building and, in many instances, the creation of quite different kinds of facilities from those that had previously existed. One of the main advantages of the Plan, in addition to its short-circuiting of the eleven-plus, is that it provides a change in schools for children at the age of fourteen, when many are ready for a new environment. It also avoids the creation of excessively large comprehensive schools by breaking the secondary program into two parts.

It is fortunate, but not really surprising, that the evils of the eleven-plus examination were so apparent. (Other local education authorities in England are now considering abolishing the examination, and some of them are interested in the comprehensive, two-tier secondary system pioneered in Leicestershire.) One father in the County refused to speak to his daughter for three months after she had "failed" the examination. A child in another part of England ran away from home and was found dead on the moors after failing to be selected for grammar school. It is no wonder that only a few of the better primary schools, where the head was an individual of strong character and liberal outlook, could resist all pressures and concentrate their energies on education, instead of on preparation for the examination.

While not all teachers in Leicestershire seem to have the respect for variation in children's abilities and in their rate and style of intellectual growth that some of their

41

colleagues do, many recognize that the pattern pioneered by the infant schools is successful and worth extending into the junior schools. The abolition of the eleven-plus examination is facilitating this extension and is allowing teachers to do what they consider best for the children without worrying about external evaluation by standardized tests. The new freedom to extend the best features of established practice and to try new ideas without being concerned for overly narrow criteria of evaluation has led to a creative flowering in primary education.

FAILURE OF PROGRESSIVE EDUCATION
IN THE UNITED STATES

Why has elementary education in the United States been evolving so differently than it has in Leicestershire? Several factors stand out clearly. First, the impact of infant school education on teaching at higher age levels in Leicestershire has had no real counterpart in this country. Second, there is a lack of deep dissatisfaction in this country about regressive educational practices that could be identified and modified. Few educators in the United States have yet realized that our nationwide standardized achievement testing program, for example, is exerting the same destructive influence on elementary schools that the eleven-plus examination has had on English primary schools. We have been too proud of our skill in devising reliable tests to worry much about their validity in terms of any meaningful criteria.

A third factor may have to do with ambition. The pioneers of progressive education were reacting against practices that could readily be improved upon. They did not need to worry in those days about whether their students would be "prepared" for acceptance by the next school in line. Entry into private secondary schools and colleges was largely a matter of ability to pay. Competition for available places and a greatly elaborated testing program have changed this situation radically, and the change has ramifications right down to the kindergarten level. Few school principals have had the perspective and strength to resist current pressures. The chief function of our independent schools, and many of our public school systems as well, has become that of preparing the child so that he will be accepted at the college of his choice, such acceptance being largely contingent upon grades achieved in school and the results of competitive nationwide examinations. The progressive education movement in the United States was limited to relatively few schools, most of them attracting middle-class children. Unfortunately, these schools have proved peculiarly susceptible to pressures for achievement.

I do not know how much relationship there was between the doctrines preached at Columbia's Teachers' College and similar institutions and what was happening in the schools during Columbia's heyday as a fountainhead of progressive theory. I suspect that practice was quite different from theory. Many ideas in education seem difficult or impossible to convey by words alone. As a result, one cannot expect too much from teacher-training situations in which there is not close contact and cooperation between educationists at the university level and persons concerned with the day-by-day conduct of classes in schools. I have recently learned of a professor of education, a man noted for his liberal outlook and his capacity for attracting disciples, who decided to check on what was happening in the schools where some of his more promising students had been teaching. He was appalled! Some of us who have followed the progress of teachers trained in new ways of teaching mathematics have had a similar experience. There are often great gaps between what one says and what others do.

I have observed some of the changes taking place in a school where parents and teachers have become increasingly concerned about standards. It is very easy, in the absence of a compelling counter-example, to be caught up in a concern for a limited kind of academic excellence, a concern that manifests itself in setting carefully prescribed "production" schedules. A few people recognize that these schedules reflect standards meaningless to the child as he really is and are aware of how destructive they can be for children. Most educators, however, take them seriously and are ready to evaluate their own effectiveness as teachers, and that of their colleagues, on the basis of "objective" tests administered to the children after completing masses of detailed busy work. I have been told that over half of the independent schools in the United States, and quite a few public schools as well, now include the results of standardized tests in reports to parents, along with the grades received by the children at school. These reports generally include percentiles by which children are compared with others at the same age level on a national basis.

Do standardized tests influence what is being taught and how it is being taught? In my experience they certainly do, although many teachers would deny that they are training children especially for the tests. There is little recognition among teachers that these tests are often misleading and inadequate indices of a child's ability and accomplishment. Our educational practices have been directed toward questionable standards that are quickly accepted mainly, one suspects, because they can be easily measured.

Recently I heard a group of second-graders from a public school in the Boston suburbs discussing the grades they had received. One child was boasting of a straight-A average; his classmates were quick to point out that he had received only a B in music! However monstrous the assignment of grades to seven-year-olds appears, it is but a logical extension of a total educational system that attaches high value to narrow measures of production.

Ambition and anxiety, however, are not sufficient to account for the death of progessive education in America. If the progressive schools had been able to maintain a viable model, it would no doubt be exerting some influence even now. I suspect that progressive education as it was practiced in even the best of schools left much to be desired. The conclusion that children would not really accomplish much unless work was prescribed in detail for them seems to have been reached by many otherwise enlightened teachers. This is why the Leicestershire developments are so important for Americans now: here is a mature form of progressive education that is working successfully on quite a large scale. One of the main pitfalls that the Leicestershire schools seem to have avoided is that of excessive planning and control of the detailed steps in the educational process. Visitors to Leicestershire can see children in many different schools handling their own affairs and productively pursuing their own interests with guidance but not constant manipulation by a teacher.

The factors that have allowed one county in England to make educational progress, while so little has been done in the states, are well worth probing. I do not find particularly helpful the comment of one English educator, "Well, we have learned from your mistakes." What were our mistakes and how can we guard against making them again?

The most common criticism of progressive education in America was that it was chaotic, that the children were undisciplined and disorganized. I apprenticed to a progressive teacher for part of my training period, and I must say that the behavior problems were formidable. Exciting things happened in the class, but it took a tremendous exertion on the teacher's part to direct and redirect the children's energy. There was more disorder and sometimes chaos than I or many other teachers could tolerate for long periods of time.

In Leicestershire we found class after class in which the children had considerable freedom and in which there

45

was seldom, if ever, any need for the teacher to step in to control behavior. Such an atmosphere presents quite a shock to an American visitor who is accustomed either to the volatility of children who have been given apparent free rein or to the seeming docility of those whose every action has been rigidly controlled. The children we saw were purposefully involved in what they were doing and were capable of sustaining their interest and energy over long periods of time with little or no reference to the teacher. We visited, one Friday afternoon at three o'clock, a class that had been without a teacher for the day. There was a normal hum of activity, which continued during our visit, and some good work was still being done. Freedom and chaos do not need to go together, at least not for these Leicestershire children who have learned how to handle real freedom. One might even hazard the guess that the disorganization so often observed in schools that are trying to be progressive can prevent children from being really free by forcing their attention continually to the process of testing behavioral limits.

INNOVATIONS IN INSTRUCTION AND CURRICULUM

Is it "national character," patterns of child rearing, or some set of hidden sanctions that enables these children to work industriously and creatively without having tasks prescribed in narrow form or having behavior rigidly controlled? Whatever factors may be operating, such classes do not spring up spontaneously without there having been someone with a pretty good idea of what he was about. I was able to visit a school that had just recently come under County supervision, and it was not completely effective. In this highly controlled room, the lid was about to blow off and was being held on by strenuous exertions on the part of the teacher. The great variation among the County schools may provide valuable clues about the extent of the transformation that has taken place in Leicestershire and the means by which it has been achieved.

Most of the activities we saw in the best junior schools were loosely structured. Children were given much latitude, not only in what they did but in how they did it. Some of the most structured work was in mathematics: parts of the Dienes' multi-base arithmetic and algebra series were assigned to the entire class, but each child was to work on them at his own pace, and the assumption was made that while the teacher would keep an eye on the student's over-all progress and perhaps even check his work at intervals, the child would work along essentially without adult supervision, using the cards and materials provided. This contrast between these Leicestershire schools and American classrooms can be judged by the fact that American children who have used the same materials have had difficulty because the sequences were too unstructured, too open-ended. The Dienes' mathematics laboratory cards ask children to see correspondences between situations that look different but have the same mathematical structure and to deal more with the ideas underlying the tasks than with solutions to particular problems. American children between the ages of seven and ten have had difficulty adjusting to this orientation. They have been "thrown" when asked to make problems of their own and to write down the things they noticed without having specific blanks to fill in. Only after they have been weaned away from a passive, dependent attitude, have they been able to handle this work effectively.

It is likely that differences between American schools and those in Leicestershire have been accentuated by the use made of prepared materials in the States. Reading series with detailed instructions to the teacher on what to do each day, supplemented by disposable reading workbooks, spelling workbooks, language workbooks, and busywork workbooks are readily available to relieve the

47

American teacher's anxieties about planning curriculum and ensuring that the children will always have something to do. (Such series are available in England, too, but are less widely used; perhaps a low per capita budget for supplies has its advantages!) While some schools have rejected mass-produced curricula of this sort as intellectually unrespectable, many teachers in American schools have filled the vacuum thus created by producing hundreds of detailed assignment sheets, which they run off on the duplicator. The point has been reached in some schools where a breakdown in the duplicating machinery or a shortage of paper can cause real panic, for many teachers do not know how to teach without the aid of the ditto machine. Somehow, Leicestershire schools have escaped the spirit duplicator craze. They invest what money they have in tape recorders or desk calculators instead.

Whatever the circumstances that have allowed the Leicestershire schools to avoid drowning in the deluge of materials from school publishing houses, the result is that they are now implementing the philosophy that the process of thinking is as important as, or more important than, the specific content that might fill the blanks. Now, workbooks are not necessarily bad; it is often possible to cover certain kinds of material more thoroughly by their judicious use than by leaving things to chance or to an overworked teacher. When children have become accustomed to the pattern of following detailed instruction sheets, however, their capacity for self-direction and involvement in the subject for its own sake, rather than for the sake of completing a number of exercises, is usually diminished. It is tempting to say that a careful mixture of detailed assignments and less structured work would produce the best results. In Leicestershire classes in which there was deep involvement in excellent work, there were few combination assignments of this kind. "You can't go half way," we were told by a teacher who had moved far toward establishing a classroom in which self-direction was the basis of organization. "Either the children are going to learn to be responsible for their own learning, to plan what they are going to do and carry through with it, or they are not." We were further cautioned that the kinds of things we were seeing did not come about all at once. Bill Hazel, headmaster of the Ravenhurst Road Junior School, warned that sometimes one had to wait months in the face of discouraging results before the real fruits of self-direction could be harvested.

The Leicestershire schools have moved away from traditional patterns of class instruction. There is a great deal of interaction among children who may be working together in pairs or in small groups. There are few large-group, teacher-directed discussions in which, almost by the nature of things, the game becomes one of trying to guess what the teacher is thinking. If one is genuinely concerned with the intellectual development of children, rather than with preparing them to "look good" on tests, it is necessary to acknowledge that formal class teaching, even by skillful teachers, must have a limited role in the primary school. Learning proceeds much more effectively when the child is actively involved in what he is doing, as the infant schools have so clearly demonstrated. Such involvement does not come about when there is an emphasis on Capital T Teaching any more than it does when children are encouraged to race through quantities of worksheets.

The Dienes' laboratory sequences are designed to remove the teacher from a position of central authority so that he can observe the children learning in ways that may be quite unfamiliar to him. They are also designed to be as open-ended as possible, as frequently asking the children to make up problems as to solve them. In some schools in the County this work in mathematics has been used successfully as an opening wedge in encouraging more flexible forms of classroom organization. For example, children typically work in pairs on the Dienes'

49

material, and when desks have been arranged to make this possible, other uses for the resulting "decentralized" seating plan have been found. I suspect that flexible patterns for learning are attained through a series of steps: the first step may be a small one, leading to a classroom still far removed from that which will appear when more experience has been gained and when the teacher develops confidence in the value of the freedom he is gradually extending. It is quite an innovation, for some schools, to remove the teacher from a position of central authority and control, if only for mathematics, because new and usually demanding teaching skills and roles must be learned. It may be that at first a sharp break from tradition is necessary, if only in a limited sphere. On the other hand, experienced teachers do not hesitate to set up teaching situations, upon occasion, in which children are grouped together because they are at a similar point in their explorations, and the teacher may work intensively with such groups.

Within many Leicestershire schools there is now an openness to honest experimentation, a sharp contrast to the rigidities one so often finds in American schools. This has probably come about as a result of a series of experiences with successful innovations. There is unusual receptivity to new ideas. Teachers and heads are not hesitant to take chances with ideas that may have merit, nor are they reluctant to criticize freely when things do not work out as expected. I was surprised, although I have known of the Leicestershire developments for some time, to learn of the extent of some of the explorations now in progress, explorations that always start on a small scale and expand if they are successful. In mathematics, in addition to work introduced by Dienes and Sealey, investigations are underway on the use of Cuisenaire rods, Encyclopaedia Britannica workshop books, Madison Project mathematics, the use of desk calculators as an adjunct to learning mathematics, and an interesting secondary mathematics program being developed by Dr. Richard Skemp. In the field of reading the County is participating in a nationwide study of the Pitman Initial Teaching Alphabet (i.t.a., the so-called augmented Roman alphabet), and there is interest in Gattegno's "Words in Color." Mathematics, reading, handwriting, teaching machines, history, science, physical education, art, music, camping, and the study of the special problems of working-class children—this list gives some idea of the range of explorations being undertaken in the County. All the research is done in the field—in the classrooms—by people whose backgrounds enable them to implement and adapt ideas suggested by others and to work out projects of their own. (The above list is not exhaustive; one finds projects being undertaken with little or no advertising!) The well established lines of communication among the primary schools and advisors enable the whole County to benefit from the experience of individuals with new ideas. Teachers not only hear about what is being done, they can go to see it in other teachers' classrooms, for visiting is commonplace for teachers as well as for heads.

Here, in effect, is a large-scale laboratory in which many promising ideas are being tested within a sound educational framework. Judging from what I have seen and from the ideas that people in Leicestershire are currently discussing, there will be few paths in education that are not explored. A surprising thing to Americans whose immediate association with the word "research" may be "foundation grant," is that there is little or no special financial backing for such investigations—mainly, again, because money just isn't available. It may prove in the long run that it is actually desirable to start in a small way, without funds from afar, rather than on the massive scale big money makes possible. In Leicestershire much of what is done is accomplished on the teacher's own time, although courses and study groups are often held during school hours. Holidays may be used for residential

51

courses, attendance at which is voluntary and does not provide "credit" for the teacher. In short, there is a continuing program of in-service training for teachers old and new as new ideas require a changing outlook.

It is inevitable, I think, that serious students of education will come to recognize that research must take place outside the laboratory, in school conditions not too different from those that can be established in the schools they hope to influence. The primary schools in Leicestershire appear well on their way toward becoming a model educational laboratory for the future.

FAMILY GROUPING AND THE INTEGRATED DAY

There are two developments in Leicestershire that appeared to us to be particularly promising at the moment. One is the emergence of vertical, or "family," grouping in the infant schools, which I have mentioned above. In schools where vertical grouping is now in effect, children are likely to remain with one teacher for their entire stay in the school, at first learning much from older children in the class who have been there for up to two and a half or three years and are therefore in a position to communi- newcomers assimilate this culture, as well as being able to cate the very real culture of the school society, helping give assistance with specific skills. There is a living heritage in these schools to which both children and staff are contributors and of which both are recipients. So real is the subculture that develops that it is not surprising to find children carrying it with them into the outside world of family and peers. In some working-class communities with little tradition of reading in the home, for example, the children themselves are bringing from school an interest in books, an attitude toward reading and probably toward schoolwork in general, which means that younger brothers and sisters enter the infant school now with markedly different attitudes and expectations than were held by those entering a few years ago. Such an effect cannot be ascribed solely to family grouping, and I do not know how extensive it is, but it suggests that these infant schools are well worth close study by those in the states who are particularly concerned with "disadvantaged" children.

A second development, which may be important in the United States, also had its roots in the infant schools. A number of classes had developed to the point where the children were so involved in their work that the distinction no longer needed to be made between one subject and another or between work and play. There did not need to be a special time for reading or writing or mathematics, because the educational framework and the materials available were such that children came naturally to want to read and write and work on mathematics, to learn the necessary skills in these areas just as they learned how to manage paint and clay and a tower of blocks. It was not necessary to schedule a time for the morning milk break, because the children were capable of serving themselves when they were ready without disturbing those who were continuing to work. Some schools have milk bars now, where children can sit down and chat with their friends over their daily third-of-a-pint.

Freeing the schedule from artificial, imposed interruptions made it possible for children to continue to work for sustained periods of time. As this method of school organization, known in the County by the cumbersome name "integrated day," was found successful in the infant schools, it was extended to some junior classes, on the theory that children used to working freely as infants could make even better use of freedom as juniors. The relaxed but purposeful atmosphere we found in some infant and junior schools certainly resulted, in part, from this throwing away of fixed schedules and allowing children to work at their own pace on tasks of their own choosing. The teacher, in such a situation, must be aware

53

of the kinds of things each child is doing over a period of time, but there is no longer the expectation that every child will do everything every day.

The matter of pace is interesting. On occasion we saw children moving slowly, even dawdling at, say, changing their clothes for P.E. There was no hurry at all here, but neither was there any sense of pressure among the children who were painting or writing books or doing mathematics. There was little tension or nervous excitement among the children.

The extension of the integrated day to the junior schools was a logical step, revolutionary as it seemed to some, and already it has proved attractive to a number of schools. The junior classrooms we visited, which were newly organized along these lines, seemed to be having an easy and profitable time of it, despite marked differences in temperament and ability among the teachers running them. The children in these classes were free to choose what they wanted to do and to carry out their work in a responsible way. The atmosphere was one of absorption, and the work done was of an exceptionally high quality. The junior schools do not yet have the rich backlog of materials and projects available to the infant schools, but the inventiveness of teachers and the open communication system among them is likely to establish, before too long, a junior school tradition similar to that of the infant schools.

ACCOMPLISHMENTS AND CHALLENGES

Many people will recognize that what is being accomplished in the best of the Leicestershire schools consitutes a desirable form of education. The County's achievements are basically honest and are not contrived to meet pressures essentially irrelevant to good learning. We in the

United States, however, have a whole set of expectations and assumptions that will make change difficult. Many teachers will be prepared to acknowledge that the standard of written English is quite a bit higher in Leicestershire or that there the average child's accomplishment in mathematics is superior to that of children from even the most favored backgrounds in the States. They may not be prepared to recognize that the attainment of such standards is the result of giving children the freedom and the stimulation to become genuinely involved in the process of their own education, instead of prescribing for children in fragmented detail what they should be doing at every step of the way and communicating, via tests and grades, a sense of anxiety and pressure about achievement. Teachers may not be able to admit that Leicestershire schools are moving in a direction opposite to that being taken by most schools here.

There will be those who will not accept the evidence of their own eyes and ears as they watch a Leicestershire classroom in operation. Children may have a zest for learning and attain obvious high standards in their work, and yet the question some people immediately ask will be, "How do their standardized test scores compare?" Occasionally it happens that a child in his last year of a really fine Leicestershire junior school moves to another county and must take the eleven-plus. All evidence indicates that with just a little last-minute coaching these children do just as well as children whose entire career in junior school has been pointed toward the examination. That these children do so well on an examination for which their schooling has not specifically prepared them could prove to be the fact that would lead many people to consider the desirability of implementing a Leicestershire-type program. It does not seem likely, though, that such implementation will prove successful if undertaken under pressure by people who might come to feel that the goal was to boost test scores a few points.

It is easy enough to be dispassionate in considering broad social and cultural influences upon our schools. It is not so easy to be restrained when one is closely familiar with what certain practices mean in the lives of individual children who become the victims of their parents' and their teachers' ambitions. When the exploitation becomes institutionalized, as it has been in so many places, it is hard to realize that there are more honest, more human ways of organizing learning.

The effect of having classes in which children must continually accommodate themselves to the teacher's train of thought and to a production schedule that specifies what is to be done in inflexible detail is to set up a series of races in which certain skills and attitudes are strongly rewarded. The production strategies successful students develop have little relation to honest intellectual endeavor and are likely to inhibit the growth of intellectual skills and attitudes necessary for creative growth in any field. Production demands greatly restrict the development of diverse styles. The daily races in the classroom reward a limited and not very valuable range of talents. Given such a system, one should not be surprised that students with real creative potential are increasingly to be found among the deviants, the misfits. The tragedy is that those who are unwilling or unable to meet such narrow performance demands will have their confidence in their own ability destroyed and will be left with little understanding of their own talents, while those who are successful have their own price to pay. There is an intellectual discrimination in American schools that is every bit as vicious and damaging as racial discrimination.

American schools have become production-oriented, nervously concerned about making things "look good." They cover up their own basic failures to educate in the truest sense by talking about how education must be rigorous and demanding from an early age. Great concern is voiced over children who are not sufficiently motivated to withstand the pressures brought to bear on them. There is surprise that many children do not seem to be concerned about meeting the standards set for them—and there is even greater surprise that it is often these children who are most creative. Not all children are ready to accept a hair-shirt orientation toward learning at an early age. Those who do conform and are successful are cheated just as fully as those who do not conform and learn to mistrust their own abilities.

A strong hope is that the present curriculum reform movement in America, operating through different channels and in different ways, may help the intellectual emancipation of children. Just the fact that school people are not completely isolated from professional people who have rather different styles and values than those allowed in the classroom is encouraging. Curriculum reform will amount to very little, however, if it is bounded by the assumption that the specialist's job is to set out the content in well organized form so that it may then be taught by determined teachers. I cannot share the optimism of those who feel that present trends will automatically bring about fundamental changes. I do not believe that we are facing up to the basic problem of classroom organization. We may be developing a better curriculum content in mathematics, science, and social studies, but unless the basic framework of the elementary classroom is altered in the process, not a great deal will have been achieved.

Leicestershire helps Americans to see just how sick their schools really are. What has been happening in the County gives strong support to the vision of people who have known that there could be more effective and humane forms of education and provides a formidable challenge to those who would try to implement their beliefs.

MESSING ABOUT IN SCIENCE

by David Hawkins

*"Nice? It's the only thing," said the Water Rat
solemnly, as he leant forward for his stroke. "Believe
me, my young friend, there is nothing—absolutely
nothing—half so much worth doing as simply messing
about in boats. Simply messing," he went on dreamily,
"messing—about—in—boats; messing—"*

Kenneth Grahame
The Wind in the Willows

As a college teacher, I have long suspected that my students' difficulties with the intellectual process comes not from the complexity of college work itself but mainly from their home backgrounds and the first years of their formal education. A student who cannot seem to understand the workings of the Ptolemaic astronomy, for example, turns out to have no evident acquaintance with the simple and "obvious" relativity of motion or the simple geometrical relations of light and shadow. Sometimes for these students a style of laboratory work that might be called "kindergarten revisited" has dramatically liberated their intellectual powers. Turn on your heel with your head back until you see the ceiling—turn the other way—and don't fall over!

Working in the Elementary Science Study, I had the

experience, marvelous for a naive college teacher, of studying young children's learning in science. I am now convinced that my earlier suspicions were correct. In writing about these convictions, I must acknowledge the strong influence on me by other staff members in the Study. We came together from a variety of backgrounds —college, high school, and elementary school teachers— and with a variety of dispositions toward science and toward teaching. In the course of trial teaching and of inventing new curricular materials, our shop talks brought us toward some consensus, but we still had disagreements.* The outline of ideas I wish to present here is my own, therefore, and not that of the group that has so much influenced my thinking. The formulation I want to make is only a beginning. Even if it is right, it leaves many questions unanswered and, therefore, much room for further disagreement. In so complex a matter as education, this is as it should be. What I am going to say applies, I believe, to all aspects of elementary education; however, let me stick to science teaching.

My presentation is divided into three patterns or phases of school work in science. These phases are different from each other in the relations they induce between children, materials of study, and teachers. Another way of putting it is that they differ in the way they make a classroom look and sound. My claim is that good science teaching moves from one phase to the other in a pattern that, though it will not follow mechanical rules or ever be twice the same, will evolve according to simple principles. There is no necessary order among these phases, and for this reason, I avoid calling them 1, 2, and 3 and use instead some mnemonic signs that have perhaps, a certain suggestiveness: ○, △, and □.

---

*I would also like to acknowledge the assistance of Frances Hawkins, who has long practiced in pre-school what I now wish to generalize over the entire elementary range.

○ PHASE

There is a time, much longer than commonly allowed, that should be devoted to free and unguided exploratory work (call it play if you wish; I call it work). Children are given materials and equipment—*things*—and are allowed to construct, test, probe, and experiment without superimposed questions or instructions. I call this ○ phase "messing about," honoring the philosophy of Water Rat, who absentmindedly ran his boat into the bank, picked himself up, and went on without interrupting his joyous train of thought:

—about in boats—or with boats . . . In or out of 'em, it doesn't matter. Nothing seems really to matter, that's the charm of it. Whether you get away, or whether you don't; whether you arrive at your destination or whether you reach somewhere else, or whether you never get anywhere at all, you're always busy, and you never do anything in particular; and when you've done it there's always something else to do, and you can do it if you like, but you'd much better not.

In some jargon, this kind of situation is called "unstructured," which is misleading; some doubters call it chaotic, which it need never be. "Unstructured" is misleading because there is always a kind of structure to *what* is presented in a class, even as there was to the world of boats and the river, with its rushes and weeds and mud that smelled like plumcake. Structure in this sense is of the utmost importance, depending on the children, the teacher, and the backgrounds of all concerned.

Let me cite an example from my own recent experiences. Simple frames, each designed to support two or three weights on strings, were handed out one morning in a fifth-grade class. There was one frame for each pair of children. In two earlier trial classes, we had introduced the same equipment with a much more "structured" beginning, demonstrating the striking phenomenon of coupled pendulums and raising questions about it before the laboratory work was allowed to begin. If there was guidance this time, however, it came only from the apparatus —a pendulum is to swing! In starting this way I, for one, naively assumed that a couple of hours of "messing about" would suffice. After two hours, instead, we allowed two more and, in the end, a stretch of several weeks. In all this time, there was little or no evidence of boredom or confusion. Most of the questions we might have planned for came up unscheduled.

Why did we permit this length of time? First, because in our previous classes we had noticed that things went well when we veered toward "messing about" and not as well when we held too tight a rein on what we wanted the children to do. It was clear that these children had had insufficient acquaintance with the sheer phenomena of pendulum motion and needed to build an apperceptive background, against which a more analytical sort of knowledge could take form and make sense. Second, we allowed things to develop this way because we decided we were receiving a new kind of feedback from the children and were eager to see where and by what paths their interests would evolve and carry them. We were rewarded with a higher level of involvement and a much greater diversity of experiments. Our role was only to move from spot to spot, being helpful but never consciously promoting or directing. In spite of—because of!—this lack of direction, these fifth-graders became very familiar with pendulums. They varied the conditions of motion in many ways, exploring differences of length and amplitude, using different sorts of bobs, bobs in clusters, bobs on strings, and so on. And have *you* tried the underwater pendulum? They did!

There were many sorts of discoveries made, but we let them slip by without much adult resonance, beyond our spontaneous and manifest enjoyment of the phenomena.

So discoveries were made, noted, lost, and made again. I think this is why the slightly pontifical phrase "discovery method" bothers me. When learning is at the most fundamental level, as it was here, with all the abstractions of Newtonian mechanics just around the corner, don't rush! When the mind is evolving the abstractions that will lead to physical comprehension, all of us must cross the line between ignorance and insight many times before we truly understand. Little facts, "discoveries" without the growth of insight, are *not* what we should seek to harvest. Such facts are only seedlings and should sometimes be let alone to grow into . . .

I have illustrated the "messing about" phase with a constrained and inherently very elegant topic from physics. In other fields, the pattern will be different in detail, but the essential justification is the same. "Messing about" with what can be found in pond water looks much more like Water Rat's own chosen field of study. Here, the implicit structure is that of nature in a very different mood from what is manifest in the austerities of things like pendular motion or planet orbits. And here, the need for sheer acquaintance with the variety of things and phenomena is more obvious, before one can embark on any of the roads toward the big generalizations or the big open questions of biology. Regardless of differences, there is a generic justification of "messing about" that I would like, briefly, to touch upon.

This phase is important, above all, because it carries over into school that which is the source of most of what children have already learned—the roots of their moral, intellectual, and aesthetic development. If education were defined, for the moment, to include everything that children have learned since birth, everything that has come to them from living in the natural and the human world, then by any sensible measure what has come before age five or six would outweigh all the rest. When we narrow the scope of education to what goes on in schools, we throw out the method of that early and spectacular progress at our peril. We know that five-year-olds are very unequal in their mastery of this or that. We also know that their histories are responsible for most of this inequality, utterly masking the congenital differences except in special cases. This is the immediate fact confronting us as educators in a society committed, morally and now by sheer economic necessity, to universal education.

To continue the cultivation of earlier ways of learning, therefore, to find *in school* the good beginnings, the liberating involvements that will make the kindergarten seem a garden to a child and not a dry and frightening desert— this is a need that requires much emphasis on the style of work I have called ◯, or "messing about." Nor does the garden in this sense end with a child's first school year, or his tenth, as though one could then put away childish things. As time goes on, through a good mixture of this with other phases of work, "messing about" evolves with the child and thus changes its quality. It becomes a way of working that is no longer childish, though it remains always childlike, the kind of self-disciplined probing and exploring that is the essence of creativity.

The variety of the learning—and of inhibition against learning—that children bring from home when school begins is great, even within the limited range of a common culture with common economic background (or, for that matter, within a single family). Admitting this, if you then cast your mind over the whole range of abilities and backgrounds that children bring to kindergarten, you see the folly of standardized and formalized beginnings. We are profoundly ignorant about the subtleties of learning, but one principle ought to be asserted dogmatically—that some continuity in the content, direction, and style of learning must be provided. Good schools begin with what children have *in fact* mastered, probe next to see what *in fact* they are learning, and continue with what *in fact* sustains their involvement.

63

△ PHASE

When children are led along a common path, there are always advanced ones and always stragglers. Generalized over the years of school routine, this lends apparent support to the still widespread belief in some fixed, inherent levels of "ability," and to the curious notions of "under-" and "over-achievement." Now, if a teacher introduces a topic with a good deal of "messing about," the variance does not decrease, it increases. From a conventional point of view, this means the situation gets worse, not better. But I say it becomes better, not worse. If after such a beginning you pull in the reins and "get down to business," some children will have happened to go your way already, and you will believe that you are leading them successfully. Others will have begun, however, to travel along quite different paths, and you have to tug hard to pull them back on to yours. Through the eyes of these children you will see yourself as a dragger, not a leader. We saw this clearly in the pendulum class I referred to; the pendulum is a thing that seems deceptively simple but it raises many questions in no particular, necessary order. So the path each child chooses is his best path.

The result is obvious, but it took me time to see it. If a teacher once lets children evolve their own learning, along paths of their choosing, then he must see it through and *maintain* the individuality of their work. One cannot begin that way and then say, in effect, "That was only a teaser," thus using one's adult authority to devalue what the children themselves, in the meantime, have found most valuable. So if "messing about" is to be followed by, or evolve into, a stage where work is more externally guided and disciplined, there must be at hand what I call "multiply programmed" material—material that contains written and pictorial guidance of some sort for the student, but designed for the greatest possible variety of topics, ordering of topics, and so forth, so that for almost any given way into a subject that a child may evolve on his own, material is available that he will recognize as helping him farther along that very way.

Heroic teachers have sometimes prepared this on their own, but it is obviously one of the areas where designers of curriculum materials can be of enormous help. Designing materials with a rich variety of choices for teacher and child frees the teacher from the role of "leader-dragger" along a single preconceived path and gives the teacher encouragement and real logistical help in diversifying the activities of the group. Such material includes good equipment, but, above all, it suggests many beginnings, paths from the familiar into the unknown. We did not have this kind of material ready for the pendulum class I spoke about earlier and still do not have it. I intend to work at it and hope others will too.

A special day in the history of that pendulum class brought home to me what was needed. My teaching partner was away (I had been the observer, she the teacher). To shift gears for what I saw as a more organized phase of our work, I announced that for a change we were all going to do the same experiment. I said it firmly, and the children were, of course, obliging. Yet, I saw an immediate loss of interest in part of the class as soon as my experiment was proposed. It was designed to raise questions about the *length* of a pendulum when the bob is multiple or odd-shaped. Some had come upon the germ of that question already; others had had no reason to.

As a college teacher I have tricks, and they worked here as well, so the class went well, in spite of the unequal readiness to look at "length." We hit common ground with rough blackboard pictures of many pendulums hanging from a common support, differing in length and in the shape and size of bobs. Which ones would "swing together"? Because their eyes were full of real pendulums, I think, the children could *see* those blackboard pictures swinging! A colloquium evolved that harvested the crop

65

of insights that had been sowed and cultivated in previous weeks. I was left with a hollow feeling, nevertheless. It went well where, and only where, the class found common ground, whereas in "messing about" all things had gone uniformly well. In staff discussion afterward, it became clear that we had skipped an essential phase of our work, the one I am now calling $\triangle$ phase or multiply programmed.

There is a common opinion, floating about, that a rich diversity of classroom work is possible only when a teacher has small classes. "Maybe *you* can do that; but you ought to try it in my class of forty-three!" I want to be the last person to belittle the importance of small classes, but in this particular case, the statement ought to be made that in a large class one cannot afford *not* to diversify children's work—or rather *not* to allow children to diversify, as they inevitably will if given the chance. So-called "ability grouping" is a popular answer today, but it is no answer at all to the real questions of motivation. Groups lumped as equivalent with respect to the usual measures are just as diverse in their tastes and spontaneous interests as unstratified groups! The complaint that in heterogeneous classes the bright ones are likely to be bored because things go too slow for them ought to be met with another question: "Does that mean that the slower students are *not* bored?" When children have no autonomy in learning, everyone is likely to be bored. In such situations the overworked teachers have to be "leader-draggers," always playing the role of Fate in the old Roman proverb: "The Fates lead the willing; the unwilling they drag."

"Messing about" produces the early and indispensable autonomy and diversity. It is good—indispensable—for the opening game but not for the long middle game, where guidance is needed to lead the willing! To illustrate once more from my example of the pendulum, I want to produce a thick set of cards—illustrated cards in a central file or single sheets in plastic envelopes—to cover the following topics among others: (1) relations of amplitude and period; (2) relations of period and weight of bob; (3) how long is a pendulum (odd-shaped bobs)?; (4) coupled pendulums, compound pendulums; (5) the decay of the motion (and the idea of half-life); (6) string pendulums and stick pendulums—comparisons; (7) underwater pendulums; (8) arms and legs as pendulums (dogs, people, and elephants); (9) pendulums of other kinds—springs, etc.; (10) bobs that drop sand for patterns and graphs; (11) pendulum clocks; (12) historical materials, with bibliography; (13) cards of questions relating to filmloops available in class or library; (14) cross-reference cards to other topics, such as falling bodies, inclined planes, and so forth; and (15–17) blank cards to be filled in by classes and teachers for each other.

This is only an illustration; of course, each area of elementary science will have its own style of "multiply programmed" materials. The ways of organizing these materials will depend on the subject. There should always be those blank cards, outnumbering the rest.

There is one final warning. Such a file is properly a kind of programming—but it is *not* the base of rote or merely verbal learning, taking a child little step by little step through the adult maze. Each item is simple and pictorial, and it guides by suggesting further explorations, not by replacing them. The cards are only there to relieve the teacher from a heroic task. And they are only there because there are apparatus, film, a library, and raw materials from which to improvise.

☐ *PHASE*

In the class discussion I referred to about the meaning of *length* when applied to a pendulum, I was reverting back to the college teacher habit of lecturing; I said the lesson went very well in spite of the lack of multiply programmed background, one that would have taken more of the class through more of the basic pendulum topics. It was not, of course, a lecture in the formal sense. It was question-and-answer, with discussion between children as well. But still, I was guiding it and fishing for the good ideas that were ready to be born, and I was telling a few stories, for example, about Galileo. Others could do it better. I was a visitor and am still only an amateur. I was successful then only because of the long buildup of latent insight, the kind of insight that Water Rat had stored up from long afternoons of "messing about" in boats. It was more than he could ever have been told, but it gave him much to tell. Latent insight is not all there is to learning, of course, but it is the magical part, the part most often killed in school. Its language is not yet that of the textbook, but with it, even a dull-looking textbook can come alive.

One boy thought the length of a pendulum should be measured from the top to what he called "the center of gravity." If a class has not done a lot of work with balance materials, this phase, for most children, would be only the handle of an empty pitcher, or a handle without a pitcher at all. So I do not insist on the correct term. Incidentally, it is not quite correct physics anyway, as those will discover who work with the stick pendulum. Although different children had specialized differently in the way they worked with pendulums, there were common elements, increasing with time, that would sustain a serious and extended class discussion.

It is this pattern of discussion I want to emphasize by calling it a separate ☐ phase. It includes lecturing, formal or informal. In the above situation, we were all quite ready for a short talk about Galileo and ready to ponder the question whether there was any relation between the way unequal weights fall together and the way they swing together when hanging on strings of the same length. Here we were approaching a question—a rather deep one not to be disposed of in fifteen minutes—of theory, going from the concrete perceptual to the abstract conceptual. I do not believe that such questions will come alive either through the early "messing about" or through the multiply programmed work with guiding questions and instructions. I think they come primarily with discussion, argument, the full colloquium of children and teacher. Theorizing in a creative sense needs the content of experience and the logic of experimentation to support it. But these do not automatically lead to conscious abstract thought. Theory is square!

We of the Elementary Science Study are probably identified in the minds of those acquainted with our work (and sometimes perhaps in our own minds) with the advocacy of laboratory work and a free, fairly ○ style of laboratory work at that. This may be right and justified by the fact that prevailing styles of science teaching are □ most of the time, much too much of the time. But what we criticize for being too much and too early, we must work to readmit in its proper place.

CONCLUSIONS

I have discussed ○, △, and □ in that order, but I do not advocate any rigid order; such phases may be mixed in many ways and ordered in many ways. Out of a colloquium comes new "messing about." Halfway along a programmed path, new phenomena are accidentally observed. In an earlier, more structured class, for instance, two girls were trying obediently to reproduce some phenomena of coupled pendulums I had demonstrated. I heard one say, "Ours isn't working right." Of course pendulums never misbehave; it is not in their nature. They always do what comes naturally, and in this case, they were executing a curious dance of energy transference, promptly christened the "twist." It was a new phenomenon, which I had not seen before, nor had several physicists to whom,

69

in my delight, I later showed it. Needless to say, this led to a good deal of "messing about," right then and there.

What I have been concerned to say is only that there are, as I see it, three major phases of good science teaching; that no teaching is likely to be optimal that does not mix all three; and that the most neglected is the one that made Water Rat go dreamy with joy when he talked about it. At a time when the pressures of prestige education are likely to push children to work like hungry laboratory rats in a maze, it is good to remember that their wild, watery cousin, reminiscing about the joys of his life, uttered a profound truth about education.

SOME THOUGHTS ON INTEGRITY

by Anthony Kallet

Written in 1965, while Mr. Kallet was serving in the Leicestershire Education Department's Advisory Section, these notes on how gifted children tend to approach learning present important implications for how classrooms ought to be organized.

Thinking about some imaginative, gifted children I know, it strikes me that one characteristic they share is a remarkable intellectual honesty. They seem to sense the integrity of the processes of discovery. Knowing and not knowing are recurrent points on many paths, and the children know they are capable of traveling in many directions. Answers are problems and, knowing this, they seem well able to tolerate and admit incomplete knowledge. Because their explorations have often led to the discovery of interesting new problems, they are motivated to explore further. Through exploration these children gradually gain a sense of which directions are most rewarding for them.

These gifted children seldom engage in word-juggling to cover up lack of knowledge. If they are not sure, they do not hesitate to qualify what they say. If they are stating opinions, they make clear that what they are saying is their point of view. "I think" and "It seems to me" are phrases natural to them. Such honesty, in the face of a world that provides few stopping places or few certainties, may underlie an important kind of giftedness. Most young children have such an honesty; they will ask any question, share any preception, make any comment—at least until they begin to sense that not all their questions, perceptions and comments are considered to be acceptable. Can it be this kind of honesty that often makes it seem that there are so many more alert, intelligent five-year-olds than there are ten-year-olds?

Perhaps the intelligent-appearing child is different from his peers less in terms of an innate capacity to think about his experiences than in terms of his willingness to face honestly their complexity, to ask and follow up questions that flow from his uncertainties and wonderings. Any child who habitually follows each question with another and who feels free to ask questions of people, of things, and of himself will quickly begin to look different than a child who is less venturesome. The difference will appear in many ways. On the surface, the questioning child may appear to have arrived at many more "answers" than the non-questioning one. More important, he will appear to be a continuously curious being for whom the process of finding out seems as important as the results that emerge. He will be a child for whom the act of exploration is the source of greatest satisfaction. Such a child will often appear to have considerable confidence in his own style of thinking, confidence less in what he knows than in the ways he learns.

School is not typically the place for unfettered exploration. It is not often an easy place in which to share one's perceptions of the world and oneself in it. It is frequently a place where answers are rated above all else, where value judgments about questions are always being made, and where questions that seem not to have answers are implicitly ruled out. The kind of evaluation of thinking that leads to categories such as "right" and "wrong" and "good" and "bad" may be foreign to a child until it is introduced by other people. Until he is told that question A is better than question B, he may pursue the one that seems to him to offer the most hope of an interesting re-organization. In doing so he may become able to evaluate his own questions.

A second characteristic of the gifted children I have known, quite as striking as their intellectual honesty, is their capacity to accept or reject other people's attempts to help them in their learning, in accordance with their personal sense of direction. This is not easy to do. The child who is going to remain gifted must learn early the importance of self-reliance but equally the importance of asking for and accepting help while developing the ability to assess it. If on occasion the question another person asks, the lead he gives, does not seem right, the child must feel free to reject it. The other person's task, the teacher's task, is twofold. First, he must decide whether the child needs help. Often he has merely to wait to be approached, but often he will see that the child is so enmeshed in a problem that he, the teacher, must take the initiative. The second task is to determine as best as possible what kind of help is most appropriate. With gifted children these tasks are made easier by the knowledge that if the help offered is inappropriate or mistimed, little harm will be done, since it will be turned aside or ignored.

A third characteristic of the children I know who have remained gifted is their apparent realization (conscious or not) of the futility and danger of drawing artificial bound-aries in the realm of their experience of the world. There is no clear demarcation between the child's exploration of his surroundings and the gradual process of uncovering his inner world and discovering how it is related to, and how it is independent of, the world outside. One trouble with today's schools is that they try to compartmentalize learning, to segregate expressive activities from those designed to lead to mastery of "reality" and the symbols standing for that reality. Gifted children seem to realize that explorations of things and symbols are in considerable part acts of expression. Conversely, they draw elements of external reality into the fantasies they construct and by means of this, they manipulate and master elements of their experience and construct new hypotheses. They are comfortable with their own creations, they accept fantasy-making as intrinsically worthwhile, and they are able to test fantasy against experience and to reconstruct each in terms of the other.

It is easier to say what kinds of learning situations these speculations eliminate from serious consideration than it is to say what specific models they suggest; there are many ways in which learning can be facilitated, many formats within which it can take place. Looking at many present-day classrooms, what seems missing is a freedom of movement, not just physical but, more important, psychological and intellectual. All the children are bound to one, or two, or three ways of functioning at any time. Part of the reason for this may be the barrenness of the classroom. There are so few things toward which children might move, with which they might become involved. There are so few raw materials, and the many prepared materials are so heavily scored with predetermined routes for what becomes imitation learning.

The raw material component of the environment is extremely important, provided that the associated human components make possible uses of the materials according to the intent of the child and his perception of them. By raw materials I mean all kinds of *things,* from pencils and paper to books and string and magnets and bottles and balances and boxes and mirrors and animals and "junk" and paint and. . . . Easy access to a rich environment may make it possible for a child to develop an appropriate response to outside assistance, to learn when to ask for it, when to accept it, when to turn it aside. He may be led to ask questions directly of things, and things, as well as people, will suggest new questions.

We must create classrooms in which a child can question freely in a setting varied enough so that many materials and ideas can be investigated. In these classrooms the child must be easily able to approach others, adults and children, who can help him, and to approach them with confidence that he, the learner, can ask and listen without being forced to abdicate his responsibility for, and his joy in, the results that emerge.

SOME THOUGHTS ON CHILDREN AND MATERIALS

by Anthony Kallet

By thinking of the interaction between a child and a piece of material as a sort of conversation, Mr. Kallet suggests several ways in which teachers may appropriately intervene. Examining the analogy further, he concludes that certain other forms of intervention may well be distracting and disruptive to the learning that is occuring.

While visiting an infant classroom recently, I spent a few minutes watching and working with six-year-old Karl. He was building a pyramid out of colored X blocks, which, as their name suggests, are X-shaped blocks that interlock with one another in interesting ways. Karl's pyramid grew to be about seven or eight blocks wide at the base and perhaps six blocks high with the apex placed symmetrically at the top. When he had finished, there were still several blocks left, and, after some hesitation, he started another column up one side of the pyramid. This left the apex asymmetrically placed. After further thought Karl rearranged things so that symmetry was restored. He was obviously pleased with his construction.

After we had both admired it for a while, I asked Karl whether he had ever tried making the same structure and then taking a few blocks out to leave some X-shaped holes. He didn't understand my question, so I asked him to help me remove one of the blocks. The result left him wide-eyed with excitement, and he ran off to bring over the teacher to see the hole. I then helped him to remove five more blocks, and after each removal, he called over the teacher to view the result. My role was largely one of steadying the structure as Karl eased the blocks out. I could see him hesitate before each removal, and once or twice he apparently changed his mind as he contemplated the way the structure was put together. After one near-disaster, his intuition became excellent, and he was able to remove blocks that did not serve a vital structural function. When the pyramid finally fell, it was less because too many holes had been punched in it than because it was handled too roughly during a removal.

Watching and working with Karl and later talking with people about what I had seen, have led to a number of thoughts about the relationships between materials and their users, and between materials, their users, and an onlooker who may want to participate in what is happening. I want to present some of these thoughts, not as fully developed conclusions but as starting points for further exploration.

It may be useful to think of a dialogue between a child and materials, accompanied by a second dialogue, or monologue, which the child carries on in his mind. No words need be uttered, although, especially with younger children, materials may provoke spoken commentary. At times no words may be involved at all, much of the "dialogue" being an interplay of images or unverbalized thoughts. But there surely is some sense in which materials "speak" to a user before, during, and after they are used. In some instances the user's actions prompt a response; if Karl placed a block insecurely, the structure wobbled or fell— a rather forthright kind of "No" or "Watch out." Sometimes materials seem to initiate the dialogue; the shape of the pyramid and the pile of unused blocks suggested to

Karl a further addition to the structure. There was evidence of internal dialogue too. At times I felt quite certain, in the context, what possibilities Karl was considering, and I could then see which he tried. One can obviously never know for certain what another person is thinking, but where thought leads to choice and action, some fairly shrewd inferences can be made.

Thinking in terms of child-material and child-self conversations suggests a style of approach that might be useful to the onlooker who is interested in what is happening and wants to participate in it. Imagine that you are approaching two people talking about something that interests you and you want to join the conversation. If you are hopelessly obtuse, you will simply barge in, all elbows, and will often be confronted by thoroughly raised hackles. If you have some sensitivity, you will generally listen for a few minutes to find out what is being discussed, to reconstruct some of what has probably been said, and to consider how to make your own contribution relevant. You will try to judge in advance its effect on each speaker; you will try to put yourself in the position of each speaker and to anticipate his reactions. All of this sizing-up is normally done quickly and without much conscious thought. Seldom will it be carried out sequentially as I have outlined it here, but some such process of evaluating the existing situation and one's probable impact on it often does take place.

It seems to me possibly useful to make a fairly direct translation of this process to the child-materials situation in which an onlooker wants to participate. Looking at what is happening, one can often infer what has led to it. I could, for example, tell from the height of the pyramid when I first noticed it that Karl must have had a considerable number of "Yeses" from correctly placed blocks, and it was reasonable to assume, although I didn't put it in these terms at the time, that he was having a successful conversation with the blocks. I was thus prompted to suggest an extension that might prove challenging. I introduced an entirely new element, but at a time and in a way that seemed natural, because Karl's conversation with the blocks seemed to have reached a pause. If I had felt that this was a pause following a series of failures, I might have suggested a different task or I might have refrained from intervening at all.

In order to join a conversation, you must obviously know what a conversation is about—not just the specific conversation at hand but conversation in general. You must know what it feels like to take part in a discussion. My analogy suggests that to join a child-material dialogue, one must know what it feels like to work with materials. It will also help, of course, if one remembers what it feels like to be a child. If you are used to confronting new materials, this shouldn't be too hard! A person who is not used to handling materials in a free way, who is not used to listening to them, is not likely to be sensitive to the two-way communication between the child and the materials. He may readily enough see what the child is doing with the materials, but he is less likely to consider what the materials are suggesting to the child and what it feels like to engage in this kind of interaction.

Just as conversation with other people is an active process, so communication with materials involves a user reaching out and taking meanings. It is not a passive waiting for something to happen but a probing for possibilities, and it depends to a considerable extent on what the user brings to the situation. A good teacher will have had a lot of experience with materials in general and perhaps with the specific ones the child is using, but he will rely on his own experience as a general guide to some possibilities, not as a limitation on what can be done. He should be aware that children approach materials with differing expectancies and competences and may receive from them quite different meanings and proceed in many different directions. Sometimes, because of his general or specific experience, the teacher will see connections between uses the child sees as separate, and his contribution to the dialogue may be to point out some of the connections. This is, of course, often what a third party contributes to a conversation—a fresh view of the possible fitting together of old elements.

It may be useful to think of materials as having two different kinds of meanings, following the semanticists' approach to words. To use the awkward but well-established usage, words have both extensional and intensional meanings. Extensional meanings are those that can be agreed on, the dictionary definitions so to speak. Intensional meanings are the personal associations words come to have for individuals—and they differ from one person to another. Semanticists point out the danger of using words in a discussion and assuming that only extensional meanings are involved or that we understand fully other people's intensional meanings or that they are the same as ours.

In thinking of materials, the extensional meaning might correspond to the obvious use, the use originally intended for the materials, the use most people agree it has— blocks are to build with, paper is to paint on. In a classroom a wider range of agreed-upon uses may develop over a period of time as a result of what children and adults do, and these become new extensional meanings —blocks are also weights for balances, and paper can be rolled into logs and built with.

No matter how many uses are agreed upon, however, it is important to remember that a child at work with materials will probably have his own set of intensional meanings for them. Just as in conversation it is often important to bring into the open differing intensional meanings of words, so it may be an important part of a teacher's job to discover and to encourage the development and sharing of as many intensional meanings of materials as possible. In doing this the conversations of all may be enriched, and a silent dialogue between a child and materials may, in good time, lead to a pooling of what has been discovered.

Some materials seem richer than others in providing opportunities for a variety of intensional meanings to develop. Some objects have such a dominant built-in use that it is difficult to see what other uses or meanings might develop. Materials may differ in what can be called their transparency, the ease with which they can be seen into by someone approaching them for the first time. Some extremely rich materials may be quite opaque. To take music as an example, a piano seems more transparent than a violin because the keyboard invites the absolute beginner to take action and provides some satisfying results, whereas the strings of a violin require such specialized treatment that the beginner is not likely to achieve much satisfaction. There are often things a teacher can do to increase the initial transparency of materials and thus make it more likely that children will become involved with them.

Things are not people, and although I find the social analogy useful, it must not be allowed to obscure some of the differences between things and people. One important difference may be that things are more often seen as neutral, not as adversaries. That is, one's general approach to materials does not assume that they are trying to hide a meaning or a use, although there may be an infinite number of meanings and uses there to be discovered. In dealing with people, even with friendly people, such an assumption is not always safe. In human social situations one quickly learns to be alert to motives and to the possibility of deliberate or unintended withholding or obscuring, as well as the possibility that things may not be intended as they are apparently offered. One may say to a person, "Why didn't you tell me that earlier?" With materials the reaction is more likely to be, "Why didn't I think of that before?" Perhaps another way of putting this is to say that whereas we *discover* the meanings of people, we *invent* the meanings of materials—although I'm sure that the distinction between discovery and invention is not always a clear one.

Finally, it is interesting to contrast the ways in which materials and people disagree or contradict. Materials disagree by failing to respond as one predicts or wishes. Instead of staying up, the improperly placed block falls down and thus communicates in no uncertain terms that something went wrong, that one didn't correctly understand its meaning in that situation. Whereas material may communicate "Something went wrong," people are much more likely to communicate the idea, "You are wrong." One might say that materials pass judgment only on a specific act or situation, while in many human relationships, there is at least an overtone of judgment of the doer of the deed, not just of the deed. It may be for this reason that children are often able to accept with equanimity the sudden collapse of a building they have been working on for twenty minutes, whereas the slightest social provocation may, on occasion, release torrents of tears. This is really a restatement of the fact that generally (and with many exceptions) materials—"nature"—are not seen as being "out to get you," whereas so often even friendly people play the game of one-upmanship. Another reason why teachers must themselves deal extensively with materials in the same spirit as will the children in their classes is that the perception of the neutrality of materials may be important as one observes and helps children who are using materials.

I—THOU—IT

by David Hawkins

I want to discuss children's understanding in the context of a proper education, more specifically of a good school. My topic, therefore, is the relationship between the teacher and the child and a third thing, a thing that has to be there, a thing that completes the triangle of my title.

This triangular relationship has been much talked about but too often truncated. People have made analogies between the teacher-child relationship and many other sorts of relationships. For example, in olden times people said, "What this child needs is good hard work and discipline," and that sounds rather like a parent-child relationship, doesn't it? Or they said, more recently, "This child needs love." That also sounds rather like a parent-child relationship. I'm sure that neither of these statements is completely false, but it seems to me they are both very unsatisfactory and that the relationship between the teacher and the child is something quite unique that isn't exactly paralleled by any other kind of human relationship. It's interesting to explore what is involved in it.

I know one rather good teacher who says he doesn't like children. He says this, I'm sure, with a rather special meaning of the word "like." He doesn't like children to be bewildered, at loose ends, or not learning, and, therefore, he tries to propel them through these stages as quickly as possible. I mention him because I think the attitude of love, which is a parental attitude, isn't really appropriate for a teacher. Perhaps the word "respect" might be more appropriate. I don't want to deny a very important element of affection for children in the makeup of good teachers, but the essence of the relationship is not affection. It is a personal relationship, but it's not that kind of personal relationship. I want to discuss this in the context of the kind of schooling that is marked by more frequent and more abundant use of concrete materials by children in schools *and* their greater freedom of choice within this enriched world. I'd like to discuss how the third corner of the triangle affects the relation between the other two corners, how the "It" enters into the pattern of mutual interest and exchange between teacher and child. Being an incurable academic philosopher, I'd like to start on a very large scale and talk about human beings—of which children are presumably a rather typical example.

WORKING RELATIONSHIPS WITH THINGS AND PEOPLE

There's a tradition in philosophy that always comes to my mind when I'm thinking about this kind of question; it seems to be more significant than some other traditions. It says, in one way or another, that people don't amount to very much except in terms of their involvement in what is outside and beyond them. A human being is a localized physical body, but he can't be seen as a *person* unless he is seen in his working relationships with the world around him. The more he is put in a box, figuratively or literally, the more he is diminished. Finally, when he's narrowed down to nothing more than the surface of his skin and what's inside, without any kind of relationship with the world around him, he doesn't have very much left.

The ancient Hindu philosophers expressed this definition of human nature by using the metaphor of the mirror. In the *Baghavad Gita,* the Hindu scripture, there is a marvelous image of the soul, which is said to be like "the reflection of the rose in a glass." Like most religious philosophy, this one is concerned with the problems of death and consolation. The theory of immortality is expressed by saying that when death occurs, the mirror is taken away, but the rose is still there. This image seems to me a very powerful one. It's not the same as the Christian idea of the soul, of course, but it emphasizes the thing I want to discuss, which is that a person can't be dissociated from the world in which he lives and functions and that he can somehow be measured by the degree of his involvement in that world. The soul is not contained *within* the body but outside, in the theater of its commitments.

The most precise expression of this idea that I know of in Western literature is by a famous English poet. I want to quote it because it says something rather nicely about the relationship of two human beings and the great "It," the world. In *Troilus and Cressida,* where "It" is a famous Hellenic enterprise, there is a period when Achilles is having some difficulties about the siege of Troy, and people are trying to buck him up. Ulysses comes on in a part of the play where nothing much is going to happen for a few minutes. Sometimes in Shakespeare when nothing is going to happen, there is an exchange of bawdy jokes for the boys in the pit and sometimes there is a bit of relevant philosophizing. This bit of philosophizing is relevant to Ulysses' effort to goad Achilles into action, but it has a universal relevance as well:

ULYSSES: A strange fellow here
Writes me that man—how dearly ever parted,
How much in having, or without or in—
Cannot make boast to have that which he hath,
Nor feels not what he owes, but by reflections;
As when his virtues shining upon others
Heat them, and they retort that heat again
To the first giver.

ACHILLES: This is not strange, Ulysses.
  The beauty that is borne here in the face
  The bearer knows not, but commends itself
  To others' eyes; nor doth the eye itself—
  That most pure spirit of sense—behold itself,
  Not going from itself; but eye to eye opposed
  Salutes each other with each other's form;
  For speculation turns not to itself
  Till it hath travell'd and is mirror'd there
  Where it may see itself. This is not strange at all.

ULYSSES: I do not strain at the position—
  It is familiar—but at the author's drift;
  Who, in his circumstance, expressly proves
  That no man is the lord of anything,
  Though in and of him there be much consisting.
  Till he communicate his parts to others:
  Nor doth he of himself know them for aught
  Till he behold them formed in th' applause
  Where th' are extended; who, like an arch reverb'rate
  The voice again; or, like a gate of steel
  Fronting the sun, receives and renders back
  His figure and his heat.

Tudor Text, Player's Edition, London: Collins

No Ajax, no Achilles even, can *be* the lord of anything, much less *know* his own worth, save through resonance with others engrossed in those same matters. No child, I wish to say, can gain competence and knowledge, or know himself as competent and as a knower, save through communication with others involved with him in his enterprises. Without a "Thou," no "I" can evolve. Without an "It," there is no content for the context, no figure and no heat but only an array of mirrors confronting each other.

TEACHERS AS DIAGNOSTICIANS OF BEHAVIOR

Children are members of the same species as adults, but they are also quite a distinct subspecies; we want to be careful not to exaggerate the differences, yet not to forget them, either. It seems clear to me that there are many complicated, difficult things children learn or can learn and that such learning occurs in an environment where there are other human beings who serve, so to speak, as a part of the learning process. Long before there were such things as schools, which are rather recent institutions in history, there were teachers. There were adults who lived in the villages and who responded to the signals that children know very well how to emit to attract attention from adults. These adults managed, quite spontaneously and without benefit of a theory of instruction, to be teachers.

I really need a kind of electronic analogy here for what goes on in a child's mind. Think of circuits that have to be completed. Signals go out along one bundle of channels, something happens, and signals come back along another bundle of channels; there's some sort of feedback involved. Children are not always able to sort out all this feedback for themselves. The adult's function in a child's learning is to provide a kind of external loop, to provide a selective feedback from the child's own choice and action. The child's involvement elicits some response from an adult, and this in turn is made available to the child. The child is learning about himself through his joint effects on the nonhuman *and* the human world around him.

The function of the teacher, then, is to respond diagnostically and helpfully to a child's behavior, to make what he considers to be an appropriate response, a response the child needs to complete the process he's engaged in at a given moment. This function of the teacher isn't going to go on forever; it's going to terminate at some time in the future. What can be said, I think, and what clearly ought to be provided for, is that the child should learn how to internalize the function the adult has been providing. So, in a sense, one becomes educated when one becomes his own teacher. If being educated means no longer needing a teacher—a definition I would recommend—it would mean that an individual had been presented with models of teaching, or people playing this external role, and that he learned how the role was played and how to play it for himself. At that point he would declare his independence of instruction as such and would be his own teacher. What we all hope, of course, is that as the formal, institutional part of education is finished, its most conspicuous and valuable product will be the child's ability to educate himself. If this doesn't happen, it doesn't make sense to say that the processes teachers try to initiate in school are going to be carried on when students leave school.

The image I want, then, is really the image Shakespeare was working with. One grows as a human being by incorporating conjoint information from the natural world *and* from things only other human beings are able to provide for in one's education.

I sometimes think that working in the educational style open educators like to work in—which is much farther along in English primary schools, I'm sorry to say, than in American schools—we forget the unique importance of the human role. We tend to say, "Oh well, if children just have a good, rich, manipulable, and responsive environment, then everything will take care of itself." When observing a class operating in this way, with a teacher who has a good bag of tricks, a visitor often is impressed that the teacher doesn't seem to be very necessary. He can leave the room and nobody notices his absence. If a teacher doesn't have that bag of tricks, he always rather marvels at what goes into it. It all looks as though it's very spontaneous, but, of course, that's a dangerous illusion. It's true only in those periods—in good schools frequent periods—when children don't need the external loop. When they do need it and there's no one around to contribute the adult resonance, then they're not always able to carry on the process of investigation, of inquiry, and exploration of learning, because they need help over a hump that they can't surmount with their own resources.

If help isn't available, the inquiry will taper off, and that particular episode, at least, will have failed to accomplish what it otherwise might have.

Now, I'm speaking as one very much in favor of richness and diversity in the environment and of teaching that allows a group of children to diversify their activities and —far more than usually thought proper—keeps out of their hair. What seems very clear to me—and I think this is a descriptive, factual statement, not praising or blaming —is that if a school is operated as those in America almost entirely are, in a style in which the children rather passively sit in neat rows and columns and manipulate the teacher into believing that they're being attentive because they're not making any trouble, then the teacher won't obtain very much information about them. Not gaining much information about them, he won't be a very good diagnostician, he will be a poor teacher. A child's overt involvement in a rather self-directed way, using his big muscles and not just the small ones, is most important to the teacher in providing an information input that is wide in range and variety. It is input that potentially has much more heft than what a teacher can possibly receive from merely verbal or written responses of a child to questions put to him or tasks set for him. When teachers fail in this diagnostic role, they begin to worry about "assessment."

I think this is fairly obvious. It doesn't say that teachers *will* but that they *can* obtain more significant diagnostic information about children and that they can refine their behavior as a teacher far beyond the point of what's possible when every child is made to perform in a rather uniform pattern. But, of course, they will not acquire the information, or will not use it, if they are just sweetly permissive and limp, if they don't provide the external feedback loop when they think it is needed. Teachers know children never behave uniformly, even when they're suppose to. When it appears they are, it's just because they've learned the trick of pleasing the teacher—or displeasing him if they're all on strike!—and then he isn't able to make the needed discrimination.

But I think the real importance of teacher-intervention comes out in situations where a child is not involved in very many things, is not responsive to anything provided. That child may be a problem who doesn't give much information, who is tight and constrained, who is often called "good." But one may observe little inklings or suggestions of interest and involvement, one may have hunches about what might prove absorbing to him. If a teacher has enough of these hunches and enough persistence, he will find *something* that works, and when he does, he will have laid the basis for a new relationship between himself and that child—this is the thing that is really important.

The rest is good and important and not too hard to describe: when children are being diverse in what they're doing and selective in what they're doing, when the teacher is giving them genuine alternatives as to what they can do, then he is bound to elicit much more knowledge of them from reading the language of their behavior. Of course, a teacher certainly isn't going to succeed all the time with every child in this diagnostic and planning process. There are going to be several misses for every hit, but one must just say to himself, "Well, let's keep on missing, and the more I miss, the more I'll hit." The importance of the "I-Thou" relationship between the teacher and the child is that the child learns something about the adult, which can be described with words like "confidence," "trust," and "respect." The teacher has done something for the child he could not do for himself, and the child knows it. He's involved in something new that has proved engrossing to him. If he thus learns that he has the competence to do something that he didn't know he could do, then, the teacher has been a very crucial figure in his life. He has provided that external loop, that external feedback, that the child couldn't provide for himself; he then values the one who provides the thing provided.

What is the feeling one has toward a person who does this? It needn't be what is called love, but it certainly *is* what is called respect. A person is valued because he is uniquely useful in helping another individual on with his own life. "Love" is, perhaps, a perfectly good word, too, but it has a great variety of meanings and has been vulgarized, not least by psychological theory.

A JOINT TEACHER-CHILD INVOLVEMENT WITH "IT"

With different children the relationship that develops with the same teacher will be different just because they are different children. When *you* give a child a range from which to make choices, *he* then gives you the basis for deciding what should be done next, what further opportunities you should give him—materials and suggestions that are responsive to his earlier choices and that may amplify their meaning and deepen his involvement. That is *your* decision. It's dependent on *your* goals, it's something you are responsible for—not in an authoritarian way but you do have to make a decision, and it's your decision, not the child's. If it's a decision to let him alone, you are just as responsible as if it's a decision to intervene.

The investment in a child's life that is made in this way by an adult, the teacher in this case, is something that adds to and in a way transforms the interests the child develops spontaneously. If, as sometimes happens, a child becomes particularly interested in a variation on a soap bubble theme that has already been given him, the teacher can just happen to put nearby some other things that might not at first seem related to soap bubbles—perhaps some geometrical wire cubes, tetrahedra, helices, or wire with a soldering iron. Soap bubbles are almost bound to catch the fancy of many human beings, including children.

What do they have? Well, they have a certain formal geometrical elegance. They have color; when looked at in the right kind of light, marvelous interference colors can be seen. Such a trap is bristling with invitations and questions. Some children will sample it and walk on; but some will be hooked by it, will become very involved with it.

This kind of involvement is terribly important, I think. It's aesthetic, or it's mathematical, or it's scientific. It's all of these potentially and none of them exclusively. The teacher makes possible this relation between the child and "It," just by having "It" in the room; for the child even this brings the teacher as a person, a "Thou," into the picture. For the child this is not merely something fun to play with, exciting and colorful, and that has associations with many other sorts of things in his experience; it's also a basis for communication with the teacher on a new level and with a new dignity.

Until a child is going on his own, the teacher can't treat him as a person who is going on his own, cannot let him be mirrored where he may see himself as investigator or craftsman. Until a child is an autonomous human being who is thinking his own thoughts and making his own unique, individual kinds of self-expression out of them, there isn't anything for the teacher to respect, except a potentiality. So the first act in teaching, it seems to me, the first goal necessary to all others, is to encourage this kind of engrossment. Then the child comes alive for the teacher as well as the teacher for the child. They have a common theme for discussion, they are involved together in the world.

I had always been awkward in certain kinds of situations with young children. I didn't know them very well and had sort of forgotten that I'd once been one, as adults mostly do. I remember being very impressed by the way some people, in an encounter with a young child, seem automatically to gain acceptance, while other people, in apparently very friendly encounters with the same child, produce real withdrawal and, if they persist, fear and even terror. It's traumatic, and I think we all know what it feels like. I came to realize (I learned with a good teacher) that one of the very important factors in this kind of situation is that there has to be some third thing of interest to the child *and* to the adult, in which they can join in outward projection. Only this creates a possible stable bond of communication, of shared concern.

My most self-conscious experience of this kind of thing occurred a few years ago when I found myself with two very small tykes who had come with me and my wife to the hospital to bring home their mother, who had just had a third baby. The father was ill, and there was already some anxiety. With Frances Hawkins they were fine; indeed, it was she who had earlier been my teacher in this art. They were perfectly happy with us together, but they had never been with me alone. Suddenly a nurse announced in a firm voice that children could not go beyond a certain point, so my wife had to go ahead, and we three had to stay behind. It was one of those moments when I could have had a fairly lively scene on my hands. Not being an adept, I thought quite consciously of the triangular principle. There had to be some third thing that wasn't "I" and the two children; otherwise we were all going to be laid waste. And there wasn't anything! I looked around, and there was a bare hospital corridor. But on one wall was a collection of photographs of some recent banquet that had been given for a donor, so in desperation I picked up the children, rushed over to the photographs, and said, "look!" I'm sure many readers would know how to handle this kind of situation; but, I must confess, for me it was a great triumph. It was a demonstration, if an oddly mechanical one, of a consciously-held principle—and it worked.

It seems to me that this kind of episode, in itself trivial

and superficial, can symbolize a lot that is important in terms of the teacher-child relationship, namely, the common interest, the common involvement in subject matter. Of course, one never really deceives children in important matters, so this interest can't long be feigned, as it was in my story. If one can't find something interesting, or tries to feign an interest he doesn't have, the involvement won't last. But if there is common interest, it may last and may evolve. A teacher needs to be capable of noticing what a child's eyes notice and capable of interpreting the words and acts by which he tries to communicate with you; it may not be in adult English, and the reception of it requires experience and close attention.

Visualize a long transparent corked plastic tube with water and other things in it, as fancy may dictate. Many years ago I would have thought that such a tube was rather trivial, rather silly, and would have said, "What's there to be learned from that?" To tell you the truth I honestly still don't know—there is so much! We can use a lot of physics words that have something to do with it; or we can talk about color and motion and other things of some aesthetic importance. By now I've seen enough children involved in this particular curious apparatus to be quite convinced that there's a great deal in it—and I don't mean just this particular tube but many similar artifacts as well as samples of the natural world. Such things can serve as an extraordinary kind of bond. The child is in some sense functioning to incorporate the world; he's trying to assimilate his environment. This includes his social environment, of course, and it includes the inanimate environment; it also includes the resources of the daily world around him, which he's capable of seeing for the most part with far fresher eyes than adults. The richer this adult-provided contact, therefore, the more firm is the bond that is established between the human beings who are involved.

CHILDREN'S INTERESTS IN PEOPLE AND THINGS

Finally, I'd like to mention something that is perhaps of special interest and takes me into psychological theory. It has to do with how human beings come to attain a sense of objectivity, a sense of reality, with how they come to acquire a stable, reliable vision of the world around them, and how, without losing their capacity for fantasy, they are able to make clear discriminations between what they know, what they have learned, what they merely believe, what they imagine, and so on. It has to do with how they are able to keep straight orders and kinds of belief and credibility. This is one of the most important accomplishments of a human being.

It seems to me that for some children, and not for others, this capacity for fitting things together into a coherent whole or pattern comes first mostly in terms of their relations with the human world, while for other children, it comes first mostly in their relations with the inanimate world.

The capacity for synthesis, for building a stable framework within which many episodes of experience can be put together coherently, comes with the transition from autistic behavior to exploratory behavior. The first is guided by a schedule that is surely inborn and is connected with satisfaction of definite infant needs. The second has a different style and is not purposive in the same way, not aimed at a predetermined end-state. Its satisfaction, its reinforcement as a way of functioning, comes along the way and not at the end, in competence acquired, not in satiation. Both modes of behavior are elaborated through experience, but exploratory behavior is not bound and limited by a schedule of needs—needs that must, to begin with, have the highest priority. A child's first major synthetic achievements in exploratory learning may come in relation to the human world, but

95

they may come equally, and perhaps more readily, in his exploration of the things of his surrounding physical environment and of their responsiveness to his testing and trying. In either case, or so it seems to me, the exploratory motivation, and its reinforcement, is of a different kind from the libidinous, which is aimed at incorporation and possession. A child's development will be limited and distorted if it does not, by turns, explore *both* the personal and the nonpersonal aspects of his environment—explore them, not exploit them, for a known end.

Most psychologists, in my reading and my more extensive arguing with them, tend to say that the roots of human motivation are interpersonal. They say that the fundamental dynamics of a child's relation to the rest of the world as he grows up stem from his relation to his mother and to other close figures around him, and that these will be the impelling forces in his life. It is, of course, in such terms that Freud built up his whole systematic theory and, although perhaps there aren't many very orthodox Freudians around nowadays, this key feature of the theory persists, I think—the feeling that the only important formative things in life are other human beings.

If people pay attention to the nonhuman world—animals and plants, as well as the physical environment, enriched to contain bubble tubes and soap film—one tends to trace this to some desire to exploit the human world. For example, a child does something because he thinks it pleases, or because he thinks it displeases, or because he's escaping an adult—but never because he wants wholeheartedly to do what he's doing. In other words, there's been a systematic tendency to devalue children's thing-oriented interests as against their person-oriented interests. It is assumed that the latter are basic, the former derivative. All I would like to say is that I think the interest in *things* is a perfectly real, perfectly independent and autonomous interest that exists in young children just as genuinely as the interest in persons is there. In fact, some children are *only* able to develop humanly by first coming to grips in an exploratory and involved way with the inanimate world.

Everyone has certainly seen examples of children who very early acquired the tricks I suppose in some sense babies are born with, but which infants can elaborate on as they grow older, tricks for getting what they want from people by planning how they shall behave. It's exploiting, and some very young children are already skillful at it. If you know such children as a teacher, you'll know they're smarter than you are because they've put a lot more investment into this kind of behavior than you have. One has to be very shrewd to cope with them. One thing such a child cannot do is become wholeheartedly involved in anything else; he has to be watching all the time to see what the adults and the other children think about it. But if you can set enough traps for him, if you can keep exposing him to temptations, if he sees other children involved and not paying any attention to the teacher, he's left out in the cold. The temptations of bubbles or clay or sand or whatever are reinforced by the fact that other children aren't playing his kind of game. If such a child once forgets his game, because he does become involved in shaping some inanimate raw material, in something that's just there to be explored, played with, investigated, or tried out, then he has had an experience that is liberating, that can free him from the kind of game-playing he's become so expert at. He comes, after all, from a species called *homo faber.*

If he doesn't free himself from manipulating persons sometime in his life, his life is going to be a sad one; in the extreme case, perhaps, it will even be a psychotic one. Children of this extreme sort are special cases, but, being extreme, they tell us a lot about what is involved in the three-cornered relationship of my title. They seek to get and to keep, but cannot yet even begin to give. The verb *to give* has two objects and only the indirect one is personal. The direct object must be something treasured, which is not "I," and not "Thou."

TEACHERS LEARNING ABOUT THEMSELVES

One final remark. It seems to me that many teachers, whether their backgrounds are in science or not, have learned something about themselves from working with children in the way that I've begun to explore. They have begun to see things of the physical and biological world through children's eyes rather more than they were able to before, and have discovered and enjoyed a lot that they were not aware of previously. They don't feel satisfied any longer with the kind of adult grasp they had of the very subject matter they had been teaching; they find it more problematic, more full of surprises, and less and less a matter of the textbook presentation.

One of the most telling stories of this kind I know concerns a young physicist friend who was very learned. He had just received his Ph.D. and, of course, understood everything. My wife asked him to explain something to her about two coupled pendulums. He said, "Well, now you can see that there's a conservation of . . . Well, there's really a conservation of angle here." She looked at him. "Well, you see, in the transfer of energy from one pendulum to the other there is . . ." and so on and so on. And she said, "No, I don't mean that. I want you to notice this and tell me what's happening." Finally he looked at the pendulums and saw what she was asking. He looked at *it,* and he looked at *her,* and he grinned and said, "Well, I know the right words, but I don't understand it either." This confession, wrung from a potential teacher, I've always valued very much. It proves that we're all in *it* together.

THE IMPLICIT RATIONALE OF THE OPEN EDUCATION CLASSROOM

by Charles H. Rathbone

Many so-called "innovative" methodologies in education represent little more than new means of achieving the same old ends. Open education, however, unites new classroom practice with new ways of thinking about children and schools and teachers and learning. The following represents an attempt to examine the underlying philosophy of the open education classroom, the end it seeks, and the beliefs on which it rests.

Unfortunately, teachers rarely write down the premises upon which they base their minute-to-minute classroom decisions. Nonetheless, by observing open education teachers in action and by reading the books and articles they refer to most often, it is possible to compile a reasonable and not too oversimplified summary of their major premises. This summary should, of course, be taken with a grain of salt, for these teachers pledge no allegiance to any codified statements of principle. Indeed, individual differences abound, and—thank goodness—there is no open education "club."

With these qualifications in mind and recognizing that open education does not operate from theory in any formal sense, I will present a general overview of the implicit rationale of these classrooms, particularly considering six areas: how children learn, the nature of their knowledge, attitudes toward teaching and schooling and the moral and psycho-emotional contexts within which learning occurs.

HOW CHILDREN LEARN

Open education views the child not as a passive vessel waiting to be filled nor as an amorphous lump of clay awaiting some form-giving artist but as a self-activated maker of meaning, an active agent in his own learning process. He is not one to whom things merely happen; he is one who by his own volition causes things to happen. Learning is seen as the result of his own self-initiated interaction with the world. The child's understanding grows during a constant interplay between something outside himself—the general environment, a pendulum, a person—and something inside himself—his concept-forming mechanism, his mind.

Direct experience, then, is considered central to the learning process; the child learns best when given freedom to explore the world around him, with a minimum of direction from others. Through "messing about" with his immediate environment, his manipulations advance from a general, nearly random *search* to a more planned and specific *search for*. Spontaneity, improvisation, and serendipity mark the start of his learning; only after prolonged exploratory contact with an object or a concept does he begin explicit verbalization about the object, his activity, or the effect of one upon the other.

Meantime, however, the child is formulating questions —preverbalized hypotheses, if you will—about his environment and about himself, and he is submitting these tentative hypotheses to immediate tests: "Will the sand stay in my hand if I loosen my fingers?" "Will the adult react if I tap her leg with my shovel?" "Will the toy stay the same size if I move far away?" In each instance the child is seen not just as a discoverer but really as a maker of meaning, an organizer of experience.

The child learning about the world also learns about himself; this self-understanding comes as a result of both his interaction with other human beings—adults—and his interaction with inanimate materials. He tests the strength and assesses the effect of his emotions by throwing a temper tantrum; he tests the strength of an arm by throwing a stone. The reaction of people and things to his efforts help him to gain a more realistic perspective on those efforts.

This view of learning clearly places maximum emphasis on *process,* relegating the immediate *product* of learning to a position of secondary importance. Even though a child's hypothesis may be incorrect, he is nonetheless learning how to formulate, how to evaluate data, how to correct and amend and revise. It is these thought processes, not specific "answers," that deserve the teacher's attention.

This view also implies a need for teachers to revise traditional definitions of "idleness," "wasted time," and "play," for who can tell what conceptual formulations hide within what might otherwise be construed as aimless dabbling?

A VIEW OF KNOWLEDGE

Open education's belief about *how* a child comes to understand is linked to its understanding of *what* he learns. The model advanced for explaining the *process* of a child's learning clearly implies that the product of his learning results from the particular interactions he and he alone has experienced. This further implies that what a child learns is not only his *but may well be his alone,* even though it closely resembles the learning of someone else.

If one truly believes that forming a conception of the way things are is an individual act based on experiences that can never be identical to anyone else's, then one must admit not only the possibility but the inevitability of individual differences of conceptualization. Thus, what two children carry in their heads as "chair" or "aunt" or "black" will never be *absolutely* identical.

Many advocates of open education hold these convictions about knowledge:

- Knowledge is idiosyncratically formed, individually conceived, fundamentally individualistic. Theoretically, no two people's knowledge can be the same, unless their experience is identical.
- Because knowledge is basically idiosyncratic, it is most difficult to judge whether one person's knowledge is "better" than another's.
- Knowledge does not exist outside of individual knowers; it is not a thing apart. The data that goes into books and into the Library of Congress is not the same as the knowledge people know. Though it can be mouthed and memorized, abstract knowledge needs a more personal referent before it becomes "real."
- Verbalization is not the only proof of the existence of knowledge. One can be said to "know" something, even though his knowledge has not yet been communicated to someone else.
- Knowledge is not inherently ordered or structured, nor does it automatically subdivide into academic "disciplines." These categories are man-made, not natural.
- The *way* people know things cannot be easily categorized. Thinking "like a chemist," "like an athlete," or "like an historian" are *not* distinct modes of cognition. Even if they are separable, open education would undoubtedly claim that a child could employ more than one at a time.
- Man does not make his cognitive way up any universal ladder; ladders are linear, restricting, and con-

forming. On the contrary, the child envisioned by open education faces a world of potential but unpredetermined knowledge that will admit to a plurality of interpretations.*

Individualization in learning, then, goes well beyond any simple notion of "each according to his own speed." Open education sees a fundamental independence of each learner from all others, from all would-be assistants, such as teachers and parents, and from all codified knowledge as it exists in universities or texts. It holds the individual child capable of interacting with and learning something from nearly any responsive element in his environment. This means toys, manipulative materials, and measuring devices and tools; it also means peers and adults called teachers.

Because of these views of knowledge, practitioners of open education have rejected the traditional notion of "coverage" as it affects school curriculum. For them, "coverage" implies that all knowledge can be sectioned off into subcategories or fields; it also implies that there exists some inherently indispensable body of knowledge that every single child should know. Both these implications they reject.

Another implication of these views concerns the relationship between spontaneity and the existence (or nebulousness) of subject-matter boundaries. Open education teachers acknowledge the need for flexibility while preparing the classroom environment. They realize that material originally selected for the purpose of teaching biology may unexpectedly extend a child's mathematical understanding, and when this starts to happen, the alert teacher will follow the child rather than the original curriculum design.

---

*For more on open education's view of knowledge and learning, see Roland S. Barth's doctoral dissertation, "Open Education" (Harvard Graduate School of Education, 1970).

Though it is difficult to adequately summarize open education's notions about knowledge and the way children gain it, there is one basic idea that recurs in all the literature. This is the idea that in a very fundamental way each child is his own agent—a self-reliant, independent, self-actualizing individual who is capable, on his own, of forming concepts and of learning. What this means has perhaps best been expressed by David Hawkins in a speech entitled "Content and Context: the Reversal of Ends and Means in Learning" and given at Cornell University in 1968:

> To describe a human being as an agent means to describe him in terms of his capacity to extract order, form, and organization from the environment in which he lives and to build, in the process, modes of behavior which are matched to that order as it is abstracted. It means to recognize that the autonomy of this activity can be muted or suppressed, but it cannot be subjected to control in its proper function. It means that your description of the human being, your way of reducing his behavior to order, is one which he can himself attain; thus you are metaphysically on a par with him. . . . It means that the causality of his actions is to be cast in the language of reasons and intentions, not that of stimuli and reinforcement.

A PERSPECTIVE ON SCHOOLING

School, for proponents of open education, is a social institution designed to facilitate the learning of individual children through the presentation of a number of situations through which children may easily and pleasantly explore and learn. School represents the larger world, small and compact. Its function is to offer and suggest, not only to inform and instruct some predetermined corpus of knowledge. In a larger sense, the function of school is to encourage exploration, to help children acquire competence at self-selected tasks, to facilitate, in short, children's learning to learn. This means learning to experiment, learning to accept and to build on their own resources, learning, in fact, to become *responsible agents*.

The ideal open education school begins, therefore, neither with societal requirements nor with the organization of knowledge but with the needs and the concerns of the individual child. As Roy Illsley, headmaster of Leicestershire's Battling Brook County Primary School, once put it, "The basis for learning should be that the child wants to know, not that somebody else knows or that somebody says he ought to know." Or, more simply in the words of the Plowden Report, "At the heart of the educational process lies the child."

That does not mean to say that the open education school has no goals in mind for the child; it most certainly does. But in certain rather basic situations traditional academic objectives are not considered to be the *first* order of priority. For example, though a teacher may believe strongly in the importance of a child's learning to do sums, when this belief is weighed against the teacher's unwillingness to be coercive, the sums are postponed. Similarly, though a teacher may hold high personal standards of performance (build a go-cart that functions well, do fractions with accuracy, read orally with satisfactory intonation, and so on), he may choose not to impose these standards in too blunt a manner, lest the child learn obedience and deference rather than learn to formulate and follow his own standards. Neither of these points should be taken to imply that the demand for perfection or the demand that children *learn* are absent in these schools, for they are not; what must be noted, however, is the balancing of these important objectives against others—against the goals of developing independence, self-reliance, autonomy, trust, self-confidence, responsibility, and the like.

Finally it should be pointed out that through its very structure open education presents to children a model of society, not so much a theoretical presentation as an inhabitable, experiential model of a world in which different people of differing ages and capacities and interests go about pursuing different tasks at different speeds. In this way, the open education classroom presents, in miniature, a model for an organically structured, dynamic, and flexible society.

THE TEACHER'S ROLE

Within this social model, open education entertains a very broad notion of how teaching occurs. Traditionally teaching has been viewed as a vertical phenomenon, an activity wherein some higher, older, and wiser person (the teacher) passes *down* certain facts, skills, or concepts to a younger, inferior, less-wise person (the student). Open education sees teaching more as a lateral interchange, a transmission not *from* superior *to* inferior, but rather *between* two persons of nearly equal status, one of whom happens to have a special need for something possessed by the other. To this way of thinking, it is the student who is most often the initiator, not the teacher, the student who makes demands on the teacher, not vice versa. It also makes it possible to consider that a single person could be both student and teacher or that the role of teacher could be fulfilled by a piece of manipulative material.

What this means in terms of actual classroom performance is that open education de-emphasizes the view of teacher as instructor, possessor of special knowledge, transmitter of answers, filter or mediator between materials and learner, determiner of curriculum, orchestrator of large groups of children, evaluator, standard setter; it emphasizes, on the other hand, teacher as trained observer, diagnostician of individual needs, presenter of environments, consultant, collaborator, flexible resource, psychological supporter, general facilitator of the learning requirements of an independent agent. This means that in open education the teacher is mainly *assistant to* not *director of* the child's activity. As Allan Leitman once put it:

A teacher of young children is in a sense a travel agent. He helps a child go where the child wants to go. He counsels on the best way of getting there, indicating the kind of currency and the rate of exchange, the necessary "shots," the books that will help the traveler understand what he sees. He warns that some places are too dangerous or too difficult to visit just now.

This teacher, then, is a student of the child, an observer of his progressive learning, an anticipator of his learning needs. His function is not to present answers nor indeed always to present well-articulated questions; his function is to offer, instead, opportunities within which the child will generate his own questions and from which he will derive his own satisfactory answers. The teacher prepares and presents places where learning is likely to occur; he himself acts as a resource within those many and overlapping learning environments offered to the child.

When he does decide to make an instructional intervention, the teacher—nearly always working with an individual child, occasionally with a small group of children who have chosen to work collaboratively at the same task—is governed by the principle of extension. That is, the teacher's principal guide to action is the child's present and prior tendency toward a certain area of understanding. The teacher's job is to help the child to move from where he is to where he seems to be headed. For example, while observing a child and some material interact, the teacher might be aware of a number of possible outcomes; rather than force any particular one of these on the child, however, he waits for the child's signal, some indication of a predilection, some leaning in a certain direction. It is as though the teacher maintained at his disposal a number of contingency plans, any one of which he might select once the initial indication of direction has been given by a child.

Adaptability, then, is central; so is the ability to view each child and each learning situation as separate and unique. The open education teacher must intervene differently each time; not only must he be able to apply different strategies to different children performing different tasks during the same day but, indeed, he may be required to be both highly directive and thoroughly permissive toward the same child with respect to two quite different areas of learning the child has entered. The basic point, in all his interventions, is that the teacher is viewing the child as someone with a capacity for doing his own learning and for making his own decisions. As facilitator and resource, the teacher *assists* this basic process, he does not *control* it.

THE PSYCHO-EMOTIONAL CLIMATE

Given these views of what schools and teachers are for, it is not surprising that a very special atmosphere permeates the best of open education classrooms, an atmosphere that seems to foster affective as well as social and cognitive growth. In trying to describe this special milieu, Maurice Belanger, Roland Barth, and I once suggested that this is:

a place of trust and openness, where interpersonal defensiveness has nearly disappeared, where expression of feeling is encouraged by others and accepted by the group. Feelings are aired freely as inhibitions are loosened and people become more and more receptive to honest observations of themselves, their own motives, and the behaviors and motives of others. As communication about these things increases, so does mutual respect and, with both, a greater capacity for toleration of difference. The result is an increase in an individual's freedom to change, if and when he finds change desirable.

The remaining question is one of causality—to what specific factors does this general climate owe its origin? One contributing factor certainly is the absence of explicit and rigid curricular goals for children. This alleviates a good deal of the "pressure-cooker" atmosphere that typifies many schools with high and rigid achievement-orientation. Another factor is the de-emphasis of competition among peers—it is more difficult, after all, to become an aggressive competitor when each child is engaged at a different task. Multi-aged grouping also seems influential; the deliberate mixing of ages virtually assures a wide variety of demonstrable ability and talent among the children. This leads, in turn, to a greater possibility for each child to see himself from a variety of perspectives. In a 1967 speech, Roy Illsley commented on the psychological effects of vertical or "family" grouping:

Awareness of each other's strengths and weaknesses is something which can be fully realized only in an unstreamed, vertically-grouped class. It leads to, and stems from, understanding, patience, and identification with the problems of others. Children who have confidence in themselves can freely admire the work of others in areas where the others may be more competent. Such confidence comes, in part, from the awareness that everyone in the class is accepted for all his merits and despite his weaknesses. It is from the children's confident evaluation of others' work, and their own, that meaningful standards develop.

A third factor contributing to the over-all psychological context of the open classroom is the teacher's attitude toward error. When error is treated as a normal, non-reprehensible part of the learning process, fear of failure on the part of the student is bound to decline, and the absence of that fear lowers tensions considerably.

Related to the teacher's attitude toward error is the teacher's attitude toward the fantasy life a child may wish to bring into the classroom. This he accepts in two quite different ways. In the first place, he avoids, as best he can, becoming a censor of a child's thoughts; with regard to a child's fantasy, at any rate, he avoids acting as the definer of good and bad, right and wrong (though he certainly may, while dealing with a fantasy, identify it as fantasy). Secondly, he accepts fantasy as another way of knowing about the child and as another means the child has for learning about the world. In this way, as with error, simple permissiveness does not establish the teacher's policy of acceptance; rather this is set by an understanding of how error or fantasy relates to other elements of the child's pattern of learning.

By accepting the child—and his error and his fantasy and his present and his past—the teacher encourages the child to accept himself. In this way the child gains self-esteem, a feeling of worth, a sense of independence—in short, a good feeling that "nobody's *over* him," excepting himself.

As for the psycho-emotional by-products of social learning, the typical open education teacher acknowledges the inevitability of interpersonal conflict within his classroom. In recognizing it, however, he also recognizes his obligation to deal with it; he does not reserve that part of growing up for recess but instead assumes that children have the capacity to work out their conflicts and anxieties within a group of classmates. This does not mean the bully is simply encouraged to act out his aggression; but neither does it promulgate the deception that the bully's neurosis will disappear simply because it is forbidden to show itself at school. As Rosemary Williams, former headmistress of Westfield Infant School in Leicestershire, has put it:

There's a reality about the situation that encourages children to learn self-discipline, respect for other human beings, respect for themselves, and respect for materials: it's a part of their living in this community called school. I don't think you can really sit children down at their desks and teach them what respect is all about. I think you learn respect by being disrespectful and feeling how much it hurts. In the same way

I don't think you can really learn about freedom unless you abuse some-
body else's or someone abuses yours. Freedom is not a commodity we
can give to children. They are born free: we can only help them to
accept the duties and responsibilities that the rights and privileges of
freedom bring.

This view of children in school, then, acknowledges
the emotional and psychological facts of living in groups.
It accepts the consequences of drawing children out, helping them express their ideas and their feelings, encouraging
them to find, assert, and know their own unique points of
view. It recognizes, too, an obligation to provide a suitable
context for these children—alone, among peers, or in a
one-to-one relationship with the adult in the room—to
thrash out and become comfortable with their own feelings. When a teacher assumes a non-judgmental attitude
toward children's work, when the multi-age peer group is
not being motivated to compete for extrinsic rewards;
when a child does not feel pressured to produce within
a given time period some product that is going to be
graded, and when there is a general acceptance—and
even encouragement—of displaying individual differences, then the psycho-emotional climate of the classroom
can adequately reflect the trust and respect implicit in the
ethical ideology of open education.

Most essential in this psychological climate is the condition of autonomy—not only the fact of it but the child's
appreciation of and belief in that fact. Being expected to
behave as an independent agent and living in an environment that assumes that every child has the innate capacity
and urge to make sense of the world and to make meaningful decisions concerning his own activities in that
world—these expectations do have their effects on the
child. They teach him to accept himself as a maker of
meaning and as someone whose choices count. They
teach, however obliquely, a self-respect and self-esteem—
and again, a view of himself as an agent.

THE MORAL CONTEXT

To the proponent of open education who holds each child to be an agent, much of the job of teaching entails trying to convince the child to see himself from that same perspective. The ethical climate established by the teacher contributes importantly to this understanding.

In the open education environment the child is considered to be a moral being. He has rights and he has certain obligations. He has a right to elect what he will do and what he shall be; he has the obligation to preserve similar rights for others. This means that while making practical decisions about such things as classroom management, school administration, and individual instructional assignments, the open education teacher may well encourage the child to develop certain interests and skills and may even suggest alternative courses of action when a child seems "stuck"; yet at that point when the child firmly decides against doing what the teacher thinks is best, the teacher often will make the decision to honor the child's position and give up, for the time being, this particular opportunity to extend his understanding of geography or whatever. To many this appears to be rank permissiveness; to advocates of open education, however, it expresses an important priority, namely, that it is more important for a child to have the experience of receiving someone else's *respect* for him and for his wishes than to have the experience of *submitting* to someone else's notion of "what's good for him."

To honor the child's rights as a human being, then, is central to the open education ethic. It means treating him with courtesy, kindness, and respect; it means valuing him as a human being whose rights are no less valid than those of an adult. Thus open education professes belief in the natural, inherent goodness of man. It believes that a child's natural tendency is to grow into a happy, healthy, well-functioning adult. Further, it believes that the capacity

112

for self-fulfillment is good, that the ability of humans to command their own educational destinies is good, that a child's search toward fuller understanding is normal, natural, and good.

It holds also that childhood is a good and a natural stage of life. Thus when The Plowden Report says, "to live life fully as a child is the best preparation for adulthood," it is not merely making a statement about the efficiency of learning; it is instead pronouncing a general commitment toward childhood, a commitment to the present moment and its many meanings. Indeed, it is proclaiming its unwillingness to sacrifice the "here and now" of childhood to the less immediate requirements of the future.

Again, this attitude is shown by the approach of the open education teacher toward an understanding of developmental stages. He utilizes his knowledge to better adapt the environment to the immediate needs of the child; he is not intent on accelerating the child's progress through those stages.

Another attribute of the ethical context concerns the obligations of teachers and schools to respect a child's right to direct his own learning. Believing that the organizing force of a curriculum should not be a structure of codified knowledge nor any finite set of skills deemed important by the society sponsoring the school but rather the child's own question-asking and problem-setting activities, open education insists on the child's right to pursue whatever question interests him as well as his right to articulate freely his perception of any issue. It perceives a child's integrity as being violated, therefore, when a teacher makes too final a decision about the appropriateness of a particular task or idea. Proponents realize that a hasty determination of what is "too difficult" or "too dangerous" or "too controversial" may well become a self-filling prophecy.

All within reason, of course. The typical open education teacher does not countenance a child's right to hit a classmate, commit arson, or demand curriculum materials clearly beyond his capacity. English schools, however, do seem to tolerate more risk of physical injury; placing more trust in children's common sense and worrying less about the possibility of being sued by irate parents, they permit children to work with sharp tools and to exercise on towering jungle gyms. In fact the entire "adventure playground" movement in England seems to capitalize on the child's penchant for taking risks and developing courage. (The English attitude toward nervous Americans is also interesting. One head has claimed, only half in jest, that as soon as apprehensive American visitors appear on the scene, the accident rate goes up forty percent!)

Open education takes a strong ethical position on intellectual freedom—freedom to inquire and freedom to voice one's view of things. Both serve to reinforce the child's sense of his own worth, that sense of dignity that comes from expecting respect. Viewing the child as an autonomous agent who directs much of his own learning, open education acknowledges his right and his obligation to take significant moral responsibility for his own acts. What he does and who he becomes are his to decide; the role of the teacher is to assist each child to accept this rather awesome responsibility.

One final remark needs to be made about the moral context of the open education class: the implicit obligation of the teacher to articulate ethical dimensions of classroom work honestly and openly to the children. In practical terms, this implies that the teacher is responsible, when conducting "intellectual" investigations (pithing a frog, for instance, or studing the practice of slavery in the eighteenth century) to make any latent ethical or philosophical issues perfectly clear to the children themselves. To do otherwise, it is argued, would teach that arbitrary divisions between "moral" and "intellectual" do indeed exist and that they should be learned and adhered to by children in the classroom.

114

FURTHER IMPLICATIONS

Six interlocking beliefs have been described: open education's view of what knowledge is, how children learn, the moral and psycho-emotional conditions necessary for optimum classroom activity, and some views of teachers and school. One could continue to separate out similar strands for special examination, but perhaps it is equally important to note just how tightly woven together these are. The principles upon which open education rests constitute a genuine and persuasive rationale—not a pretty philosophical icing but part of the open education cake itself. Though this rationale is seldom articulated by practitioners, it does in fact affect all manner of decisions they make as they go about the business of developing curriculum, organizing schools and classrooms, preparing teachers, and the like.

A current danger, especially as open education gains in popularity in the United States, is that some well-meaning Americans will seize upon a few of its practices without fully comprehending their meaning in terms of this underlying rationale. They will then learn, I fear, that educational change unaccompanied by an integral, comprehensive philosophy cannot in the long run be sustained. Nor perhaps should it be. Far too many of us are unaccustomed to the challenge of trying constantly to relate day-to-day practice to explicit statements of principle.

In the meantime, those of us intrigued by open education would do well to examine meticulously two things: the principles on which this way of schooling rest and— even more important—our own beliefs about such questions as have been raised here.

OPEN EDUCATION: ASSUMPTIONS ABOUT CHILDREN'S LEARNING

by Roland S. Barth

Mr. Barth's reflections on a single aspect of open education philosophy point out the need for further systematic analysis of the theories underlying this educational movement.

In education, as in other fields, practice frequently precedes theory. To the extent that practice helps generate theory, this is a healthy and even desirable sequence. To the extent that practice without an accompanying theory is random, disordered, and misunderstood, practice may become weak and even unproductive.

The present practice of what I have chosen to call "open education" reflects both these conditions; it is helping to give rise to a coherent educational theory, but at the same time it has been handicapped by the lack of an apparent underlying rationale. Most accounts of open education have been anecdotal and descriptive, painting for the reader a picture of what is happening to the child, to the teacher, and to the curriculum in open classrooms. Reports abound of children each day making important decisions affecting their learning and education, of children posing, solving, and verifying their own problems, of environments rich in materials, tools, and activities, of teachers no longer in the center ring but in a role supportive of children's concerns. Yet for all the growing literature on open education, few accounts have attempted anything approaching a systematic analysis of the important assumptions upon which these practices are built.

I hope that by laying bare some of these assumptions, advocates of open education will move further away from the realm of ideology, cult, mystique, or technique (which permits one proponent to say, "If I have to explain it to you, you'll never understand") and toward the more rational realm of a coherent theory or philosophy. Until an explanation is offered, most educators will remain puzzled, if fascinated, by open education.

To date, interest in open education and sources of information about it have been limited to England and the United States, where terms such as "free day," "integrated day," "integrated classroom," "informal classroom," "developmental classroom," and "child-centered classroom" are being used to describe this educational point of view. In England, two particularly important sources of information should be mentioned: The Plowden Report, commissioned in 1963 by the British Ministry of Education ". . . to consider primary education in all its aspects, and the transition to secondary education," and the National Froebel Foundation, which publishes pamphlets on a variety of topics related to open education. In the United States, the Education Development Center (EDC) in Newton, Massachusetts, has been the unofficial center for thought, dissemination, and implementation of open education. Within EDC, the Elementary Science Study and, more recently, the Follow Through Program have been the sources of numerous published and unpublished materials.

Despite the mass of information accumulating about open education, there is still virtually no rigorous research concerning its effects upon the development of children's thinking, attitudes, and behavior as compared with the effects associated with more traditional forms of education. However, underlying the more or less clearly circumscribed set of practices associated with open education there is, I believe, a set of assumptions about how children learn.

My purpose here is to make overt and to organize a number of covert assumptions about children's learning that underlie the practices and utterances of open educators. Classification will be generative, that is, each assumption will be based to some extent upon those that have preceded it and will give rise to some extent to those that follow. Though I realize not all these assumptions would be acceptable to every advocate of open education, they do, I believe, reflect the thinking of most. In fact, I have "tested" these assumptions with over a dozen British primary teachers, headmasters, and inspectors at an in-service workshop for teachers offered by the Leicestershire Advisory Centre in May, 1968, and with a number of American proponents of open education at EDC and elsewhere. To date, although many qualifications in language have been suggested, there has not been a case where an individual has said of one of the assumptions, "No, that is contrary to what I believe about children's learning."

It should also be made clear that, while I personally share many of these beliefs about children's learning, these are assumptions I attribute to open educators. It is not my purpose to assess their validity nor to answer the questions: "How does one *know* the practices related with these assumptions are in the best interest of children?" Nor shall I attempt to evaluate open education; rather, my concern will be to uncover and analyze what I see to be its salient features and to point out some of the perplexing questions associated with the assumptions.

MOTIVATION

Assumption 1: Children are innately curious and display exploratory behavior quite independent of adult intervention.

118

Assumption 2: Exploratory behavior is self-perpetuating.

The concept of motivation has always had a prominent place in theories of learning. Since such theories are man-made constructs, it is not surprising to find the intervention of adults commonly associated with the learning of other organisms. A pigeon pecks at a light, and the adult human dispenses a pellet or arranges to have a pellet dispensed; a child submits a perfect paper, and an adult supplies an "A." In these views of motivation the adult places himself in a position of both importance and control with respect to the learning organism. This seems to be a position of some comfort to him.

Open educators question whether motivation generated and manipulated by an adult results in greater learning or in just increased production. They also question whether an adult's intervention is essential for a child to be motivated and to learn. Thus the assumption that children are innately curious, predisposed toward exploration, and not dependent upon adults for motivation for either the initiation or the perpetuation of learning activities seriously challenges much conventional learning theory and raises some important questions.

The assumptions discussed here about motivation point toward an underlying sense of *trust* in the innate abilities of children, in their capacity to energize and direct their own exploration, and in their wanting to explore and learn. This implies the existence of an inner motivation on the part of children and a hands off role for adults.

A closer examination of these assumptions about motivation suggests another component equally as important as the autonomy of a child's motivation. Children may have in and of themselves the *capacity* for motivation, but motivation is realized only through the relationship of an individual to something outside himself, to other persons, or to bits and pieces of the world. That is, one is not motivated in a vacuum; one must have something to be motivated about. The source of motivation resides neither in the child nor in the external world but in the *interaction* of one with the other. It is only through the interaction of a person with something external to him that motivation begins to exist and to energize learning. One has only to imagine withdrawing all external stimuli from a motivated child to see the importance of the object of exploration as well as the capacity for exploration.

In contrast to the thinking of many educators and psychologists, open educators do not perceive adults as the unique suppliers of the elements of the external world that will release the child's potential for motivation. The world is there, and children, just by being in and of the world, have their own access to it. They can influence their own motivations and explorations just as much as an adult can. They bring things into the classroom as well as use what is supplied by the teacher.

Motivation then, which may seem from these assumptions to be internal, personal, and autonomous, has an external component over which both adults and children can exert influence. It remains for open educators to clarify the place of the adult in releasing or activating the child's motivation and of differentiating the child's control from the adult's.

CONDITIONS FOR LEARNING

Assumption 3: The child will display natural exploratory behavior if he is not threatened.

Assumption 4: Confidence in self is highly related to capacity for learning and for making important choices affecting one's learning.

Open educators assume that opportunities to explore, to try, and to fail in the absence of threat contribute to a sense of mastery and the development of a child's knowl-

120

edge. There seems to be some relationship between knowing oneself and self-esteem, and self-esteem is seen to be crucial for learning. Put more strongly, a strong self-concept on the part of the child is the *sine qua non* of open education; if, and only if, the child respects himself will he be able to be responsible for his own learning. Does this mean that schools are in some fundamental way responsible for fostering self-confidence?

It appears that open educators think of children's potential for self-directed learning not in terms of "smart," "dumb," "fast," or "slow" but rather along dimensions of self-esteem. If a child feels good about himself—if he is self-confident—then he will be capable of initiating and sustaining his own learning. If he doesn't have these qualities, he won't.

But what is self-esteem? What are the minimum components of self-confidence that would permit one to say a child has it? A circular argument underlies the reasoning here. If a child is capable of making important choices affecting his own learning, he has a strong self-concept; if he has a strong self-concept, he will be able to make responsible choices. Looked at in another way, children who are trusted to make choices may develop self-control; those with self-control are more likely to be trusted to make choices.

Open educators have given little consideration to children's reasons for making choices. Is choice by the child, *qua* choice, desirable, or only choice because of certain desirable motives? Is the choice of a child who chooses to swing a pendulum for neurotic reasons—to attract the teacher's attention or to wrest the appartus away from another child—as desirable as that of a child whose choice is directed by his desire to explore the relationship between the swing of the pendulum and the length of the string? Are the neurotic child's choices as legitimate, whatever his reasons, as those of the healthy child?

The important point here is that open educators have

121

not yet considered, let alone established, a relationship between development of self-confidence and the ability to make responsible choices about learning. So far, the two are seen as necessary to one another, but the nature of the relationship remains to be spelled out.

Assumption 5: *Active exploration in a rich environment offering a wide array of manipulative materials will facilitate children's learning.*

Assumption 6: *Play is not distinguished from work as the predominant mode of learning in early childhood.*

Children's learning, like motivation, does not occur in a vacuum. Children play *with* something or someone; they don't just play. Exploratory behavior is of little consequence unless there is something to explore.

The word "play" is often used in schools to distinguish activities from "work," but in many open schools neither term is appropriate, for the distinction between the two has all but disappeared and given way to a distinction between involvement and lack of involvement.

Yet perhaps this distinction should not be dismissed quite so easily. There are many activities in which children engage, such as learning to play the piano, which are tedious, laborious, and even painful. Others, such as playing ball, are fun, unrestrained, and carefree for most children. Both may be characterized by active involvement with materials, but they are considerably different, as any child knows. One appears from the adult point of view to be "work" and the other "play." How, if at all, do open educators account for these differences?

Open educators would admit that there are vast differences in the nature of activities in which children become involved, but they point out the rewards come from participating in and completing the activity and are not dependent on the ease of the activity. Hence, the labor of learning to play a musical instrument may well be greater than that of playing ball, but so may be the reward. Otherwise, the child would be playing ball, not playing the piano.

One of the problems open educators have in trying to distinguish between work and play or in trying to eliminate the distinction is that they have not been able to separate the adult's view of what the child does from the child's view. Young children are not conscious of a work-play distinction but become increasingly aware of one as they progress up through the grades. The work-play distinction appears to be an adult artifact. Adults have assumed that anything that is productive for children in school is difficult and often painful. If it hurts, there must be something beneficial about it. Conversely, it has been assumed that those activities that are fun and pleasurable are unproductive and usually take place in "free time" or out of school. It would seem that open educators have some obligation to make the relationship between play and learning clearer.

Assumption 7:   *Children have both the competence and the right to make significant decisions concerning their own learning.*

Assumption 8:   *Children will be likely to learn if they are given considerable choice in the selection of the materials they wish to work with and in the selection of the questions they wish to pursue with respect to those materials.*

Assumption 9:   *Given the opportunity, children will choose to engage in activities that will be of high interest to them.*

Assumption 10: If the child is fully involved in and having fun with an activity, learning is taking place.

Central to open education is the question of agency. Who or what directs the child's explorations and play? What is the origin of the problems and materials in which he engages?

Many open educators eschew any attempt whatsoever to control or manipulate children's behavior. However, in the act of selecting materials for the classroom the adult does, in fact, exercise a large measure of control over the direction of the child's learning and exploration. Ideas and concepts emerge out of activity with materials. Control of materials, then, implies control of experience, which in turn implies control of ideas and concepts. By bringing books into a classroom, the teacher makes it more likely that children will want to learn how to read. If there were no written words available, perhaps they wouldn't. By bringing a telescope into a classroom, the teacher increases the likelihood that children will become interested in the stars and planets.

If open educators really wish to free children from all adult controls, they may have to abandon the institution of school altogether. It is doubtful that even this measure would eliminate adult control of children's activities, and it is questionable whether complete removal of adult control is desirable. Most children don't have access to a wide range of materials they might want to explore, nor do they have the time and place that would permit such exploration.

The success of the open classroom would seem to depend not upon the abdication of adult control over children but upon a deliberate and conscious sharing of responsibility for learning on the part of child and teacher. The adult, to a large extent, determines the nature of the school environment; the child decides with which of these materials he will work, to which problems he will address himself, for how long, and with whom.

Since the materials for children's learning are so important, criteria for their selection are crucial. The teacher in the open school favors materials that are likely to initiate and sustain interest, exploration, and learning. For five-year-olds he might choose a set of blocks rather than a deck of cards or a picture book rather than a dictionary. Often his selection is based upon a hunch that the materials will be found interesting.

Applied purely, this criterion becomes difficult, for almost anything might be expected to evoke some interest for some children some time, be it a scrap of linoleum, a jar of mayonnaise, or a mathematics text. Hence, there is a second criterion often used by open educators: the teacher selects materials that in all likelihood will stimulate children to explore in a productive way, along a productive course, toward a productive understanding. But what does "productive" mean? It is commonly held that *any* material that fully stimulates a child's interest is productive and leads to productive learning. To the extent, then, that "productivity" is defined in terms of a child's interest and not the predetermined interests of an adult, this criterion becomes indistinguishable from the previous one.

Thus we find open educators inconsistent and even somewhat confused on the question of criteria for selection of materials. On the one hand there is confidence that any activity in which a child is fully engaged and interested is productive and will result in learning; on the other hand there is an inclination to make distinctions between "productive" materials and "unproductive" materials. The former suggests a trust in children to choose what is best for themselves; the latter suggests that adults know what is best for children. Democratic and humanistic assumptions about children—that individuals, regardless of age and size, are masters of their own lives and minds —conflict with assumptions that children do not always know what is best for themselves. This is an area that needs a great deal of clarification.

Until clarification comes, there is little hope of gaining consensus from open educators on the issue of how much to trust children. At this time, therefore, it might be better to ask and try to resolve questions of another sort. In regulating the child's learning, what should be the division of responsibility between the adult and the child? In what kinds of situations should the judgments of the older, more mature, presumably wiser adult prevail? When should the child's judgment predominate?

We need to know, for example, whether the "What am I supposed to do?" syndrome of children is a cue for more adult intervention or an expression of need for greater child responsibility. We need to know whether the fact that children seem to study the things they know and care most about is a cue to give more external direction and control or an argument for releasing a child to follow his own path. We need to know if, in giving up control over the content of a child's learning by letting him choose what to pursue, adults are not gaining another kind of control—over his motivation and participation. We need guidelines and statements of clear priorities that will help adults make decisions affecting children's learning. We need to know which of these guidelines are generalizable and which are specific to the child and to the situation.

SOCIAL LEARNING

Assumption 11: When two or more children are interested in exploring the same problems or the same materials, they will often choose to collaborate in some way.

Assumption 12: When a child learns something that is important to him, he will wish to share it with others.

Open educators emphasize the individual—individualized learning, individualized materials, individualized knowledge. There has been much talk about the interpersonal relation of the child with the teacher but very little of the relationship of one child to another; yet children come to school together, sit together, work together, eat together, and learn together. Children seem to be seen as individual learners with unique styles, while in fact they are often members of one or more groups. Is this an inconsistency? What place do other children play in an individual's learning?

The interaction of children within groups has important implications for their learning. For instance, children learn to talk intelligently through participation in group activities. The development of spoken language is crucial to concept formation. Often children understand one another's problems, interests, and possibilities better than adults do and are able to assist in ways that would be impossible for adults.

Open educators only hint at the role other children play in an individual's learning; each child is seen as a potential resource for another—just as the library, adults, and classroom materials may be viewed as resources. However, viewing of another person as a "resource" seems to place him in the position of an animate *object,* a place quite inconsistent with the prevailing humanism that characterizes so much of the literature of open education.

The dynamics among children are an essential component in any educational rationale and especially in one so conscious of personal interaction. Yet open educators have not discussed much of either the meaning for the child or the effect on learning that such interaction might have.

INTELLECTUAL DEVELOPMENT

Assumption 13: Concept formation proceeds very slowly.

Assumption 14: Children learn and develop intellectually not only at their own rate but in their own style.

Assumption 15: Children pass through similar stages of intellectual development—each in his own way, at his own rate, and in his own time.

Assumption 16: Intellectual growth and development take place through a sequence of concrete experiences followed by abstractions.

Assumption 17: Verbal abstractions should follow direct experience with objects and ideas, not precede them or substitute for them.

The elements of intellectual development emphasized by open educators appear to be the following: children need time to learn; they go through developmental stages; their thinking progresses along a sequence from concrete to abstract.

Open educators question whether the adult is the best judge of how to organize children's time to ensure maximum intellectual development. They argue that at least until adults know much more about how children think and learn, the child is a better judge of his needs with respect to time than is an adult. Open educators observe that children need varying amounts of time—often quite a long time—to develop concepts. Children need time to repeat experiences over and over again, such as lighting a bulb with a battery and wire or measuring volume with a cup. Children's exploration is initiated and directed by materials and interest and facilitated, rather than controlled, by the clock. In short, time is seen as the servant, not the master, of the child.

The fact that Piaget and others have identified and described stages of intellectual development characteristic of most children would seem to have great significance for open education and for the schools. Some educators have responded by trying to accelerate children's passage through the stages, a practice Piaget has deplored as have most open educators.

What the stages do imply for open educators is not clear. Although Piaget, like open educators, believes that children need materials to develop cognitively, there is some difference between his emphasis and theirs. Piaget has children use materials so that he can see what they are thinking. Open educators have children use materials in the hope that discoveries will be made by the children. Whereas materials permit Piaget to describe children's thinking, open educators' materials appear instead to prescribe children's thinking. Measuring devices and sand are provided in classrooms with the expectation that children will develop the concept of conservation of volume. Does this imply that all children should be required to play with these materials? Is there an optimum or logical sequence of materials that corresponds to the stages of intellectual development?

Open educators distinguish between concrete and abstract, between object and symbol, especially with regard to language acquisition. Piaget's research has demonstrated the immense difference between the thought world of the child and that of the adult—quantitatively and qualitatively. What appears to be conceptual thinking on the part of a child is often verbal association. Consequently open educators believe that children must go through a physical, kinesthetic experience before they can talk or write about the ideas implicit in the experience. They resist labelling or having children label bits of learning before they have these primary experiences. They feel that if the verbal level of thought is not based upon concrete experiences, words may obscure rather than enhance meaning. One can infer a hierarchy of thought and communication that must be negotiated in some order.

What are the practical implications? For instance, how soon after a child has had a primary experience and under what conditions can he verbalize ideas? Is adulthood seen as a period of abstract verbal thinking based upon the collected experiences of childhood, or must anyone at any age develop his ideas by moving up and down the hierarchy of experience to abstract verbalization? Is it more desirable for a child to operate from the real to the abstract or to move toward the time when he can operate in both modes simultaneously or in alternation? Is the goal a condition where the concrete becomes no longer necessary?

By holding that intellectual development can be reduced to a sequence of concrete experiences followed by abstractions, open educators ignore an important alternative view—that experience and abstraction, rather than being discrete, ordered, and mutually exclusive in time, occur simultaneously from the moment of first sensory perception—a position that cannot be put aside lightly.

Futhermore, open educators have not yet reconciled their view of learning as unique and idiosyncratic to each individual with the uniformity of thinking, or at least of the uniform development of thinking, implicit in the idea of intellectual stages of development. So far the existence of stages and the flow from concrete to abstract in the development of children's thinking have been of great interest to open educators but have not led to a theoretical basis from which decisions about materials and activities can be made.

EVALUATION

Assumption 18: *The preferred source of verification for a child's solution to a problem comes through the materials he is working with.*

Open educators believe that appraisal of a child's work is best mediated not by external authorities, be they adults or repositories of knowledge, but rather by the materials themselves. Materials in the classroom enable a child to pursue problems. They also offer information *back* to the child, information that lets him know if and to what extent he has answered his question. If he has a question about how to light a bulb using a battery, wire, and bulb, he experiments. If the bulb lights, he can probably answer his question. If it doesn't light, he can still answer his question. In either case it is the materials, the world around him, that have verified, or failed to verify, his hypothesis. In the traditional school the child has little responsibility or opportunity for participating in the assessment of his work. Open educators, on the other hand, believe that the child should become as independent and as instrumental in assessing his behavior as possible and as dependent upon the materials and the situation as is necessary.

The problem is not simply one of determining the ultimate source of authority for assessment of the child's learning but rather under what conditions an adult should become a source of authority for a child and under what conditions the "world" should provide this authority. Obviously there are questions a child may ask that cannot be answered or verified by his direct experience.

For open educators, an important goal is to help the child learn to make discriminations between questions he can ask and answer for himself and those for which he must draw upon external authorities. The asking of the

131

question and the assessment of the result, then, are as important to a child's learning as coming up with the answer.

Assumption 19: *Errors are necessarily a part of the learning process; they are to be expected and even desired for they contain information essential for further learning.*

Assumption 20: *Those qualities of a person's learning that can be carefully measured are not necessarily the most important.*

Assumption 21: *Objective measures of performance may have a negative effect upon learning.*

Assumption 22: *Evidence of a child's learning is best assessed intuitively, by direct observation.*

Assumption 23: *The best way of evaluating the effect of the school experience on the child is to observe him over a long period of time.*

Assumption 24: *The best measure of a child's work is his work.*

Learning may be thought of as the effort to adopt appropriate or "correct" responses to specific situations. In striving toward this end, a child is bound to make a number of inappropriate or incorrect responses, from his or from someone else's point of view. Open educators seek to remove from children's mistakes the moral onus, the connotations of bad or wrong, and instead help children to look at the function their mistakes may serve in directing subsequent learning, in much the same way a scientist uses his mistakes. They believe that the mandate of the teacher is not to have children avoid errors but rather to have them learn to utilize the information errors contain.

Thus, not only would it be unnecessary but perhaps undesirable for adults to prevent children from making mistakes. Such intervention would cut off avenues of exploration—perhaps blind alleys—and thereby prevent children from discovering for themselves their own limitations in thinking as well as their abilities. Presumably, if a considerable element of danger to self or material were involved, the teacher would not hesitate to intervene. As with many other principles, there is a fine line here— when is it in the child's best interest to ward off a mistake and when is his learning better served by allowing him to make that mistake?

Open educators are reluctant to use children's correct and incorrect responses for purposes of placement, promotion, testing, or grading. They feel that to use a child's mistakes in these ways is inconsistent and hypocritical. This points up a serious weakness of open education practice to date—the inability and/or unwillingness to measure in any objective and systematic way the various important outcomes of children's experiences in school. This reluctance often finds expression in statements of humility and helplessness with respect to evaluation and in a conviction that important things are happening to children that need not and cannot be made known to adults with existing instruments. Such changes, it is held, will not show up in objective tests over a short span of time. There is a feeling that distilling or symbolizing a child's behavior, accepting any measure of his performance less than his total work, distorts the behavior and perhaps interferes with learning as well. Reluctance to evaluate may also be due to a decision to spend time facilitating behavior rather than measuring it, if one must choose between the two.

Open educators' ideas about evaluation reflect a profound trust in the human being, in the capacity of one to judge the performance of another, albeit intuitively. Eval-

133

uation is not distinguished from teaching or learning. There is no special time set aside for it because it is going on all the time. A good teacher cannot absolve himself from it. One can appreciate reliance upon subjective judgments and the human quality that is thereby retained, but is it really necessary to collect everything about a person before one can assess his learning? Is there no middle ground between giving objective tests and recording total behavior?

Although open educators reflect a wide range of viewpoints about testing and evaluation, they convey little of what evaluation is, whether it is desirable, or how it may best be carried out. Is testing by any objective means inherently undesirable, or is it just the imperfect existing instruments that are undesirable? Is the concept of evaluation bad, or is it that evaluation implies a clear statement of goals and objectives against which a child's performance can be evaluated? Is such a statement of objectives unpleasant for open educators because they aren't sure they know what their objectives are or because their objectives cannot be expressed in conventional ways? It is clear that open educators are uncomfortable when talking about evaluation. Unfortunately, their generalized discomfort obscures specifically what it is that they are uncomfortable about.

CONCLUSION

The state of thought surrounding open education is still primitive. The foregoing assumptions about learning are hunches, based largely upon impressions, gut feelings, emotional responses, and informal observations in classrooms. Collectively, the assumptions do not constitute a coherent system or philosophy. There are inconsistencies and voids; there is little supporting research. Indeed, some of these assumptions, such as number 7, "Children have both the right and the competence to make significant decisions concerning their own learning," are all but impossible to test and validate.

It is my hope that this attempt at articulating open educators' assumptions about learning will lead to a more critical and complete explication. However, one cannot lightly push aside the possibility that such an effort may prove dangerous. Any effort to clarify a phenomenon as fundamental and as complex as open education introduces a disturbing dilemma: at best such an attempt can be only tentative, incomplete, and subjective; at worst it can be misunderstood, only partially understood, or misused. Furthermore, articulating these assumptions can have the effect of foreclosing and restricting the development within each individual of his *own* thinking about children and learning. In short, there is considerable danger that by attempting to make explicit the assumptions underlying open education, one can do more harm than good. As William Hull has put it (in a personal correspondence of May 1969), "I would prefer that people be fascinated and puzzled than to think they understand something which they don't."

And yet the alternative horn of this dilemma represents, in my judgment, an even less tenable and responsible position. To do nothing is to perpetuate the mystique, romanticism, and confusion that so envelops open education today. To make no attempt at clarification is to sanction the haphazard efforts of many who are already trying to adopt the practices and *appearances* of open education, with little or no understanding of acceptance of the beliefs about learning that attend those practices.

To draw attention to these assumptions, for some, then, may terminate interest in open education. All to the good; a well organized, consistent, authoritarian classroom, for example, probably has a far less harmful influence upon children than a sloppy, permissive, and chaotic, although well-intentioned, attempt at an open classroom in which teacher and child must live with contradiction and conflict. For others, awareness of these assumptions may stimulate confidence and competence in their attempts to change what happens to children in school. In any case, this attempt at explication will have been worthwhile if it provokes the educator to become more conscious of, to examine, and to develop his own assumptions about children and learning. When he is sure of what he believes, all will profit.

THE PLOWDEN REPORT:

TWO EXCERPTS

In the fall of 1966, the Central Advisory Council for Education (England) submitted to the government a comprehensive study of children and their primary schools. This report, soon to be known as the Plowden Report (after Lady Bridget Plowden, Chairman of the commission), took note of the emerging informal classroom by describing its practices and setting forth its apparent rationale. Following are two excerpts taken from volume I of Children and Their Primary Schools: A Report of the Central Advisory Council for Education: *The first is a general discussion of the purpose of school; the second describes how children learn while in the school setting.*

A school is not merely a teaching shop, it must transmit values and attitudes. It is a community in which children learn to live first and foremost as children and not as future adults. In family life children learn to live with people of all ages. The school sets out deliberately to devise the right environment for children, to allow them to be themselves, and to develop in the way and at the pace appropriate for them. It tries to equalize opportunities and to compensate for handicaps. It lays special stress on individual discovery, on firsthand experience, and on opportunities for creative work. It insists that knowledge does not fall into neatly separate compartments and that work and play are not opposite but complementary. A child brought up in such an atmosphere at all stages of his education has some hope of becoming a balanced and mature adult and of being able to live in, to contribute to, and to look critically at the society of which he forms a part. Not all primary schools correspond to this picture, but it does represent a general and quickening trend.

Some people, while conceding that children are happier under the modern regime and perhaps more versatile, question whether they are being fitted to grapple with the world they will enter when they leave school. This view is worth examining because it is quite widely held, but we think it rests on a misconception. It isolates the long-term objective, that of living in and serving society, and regards education as being at all stages recognizably and specifically a preparation for this. It fails to understand that the best preparation for being a happy and useful man or woman is to live fully as a child. Finally, it assumes, quite wrongly, that the older virtues, as they are usually called, of neatness, accuracy, care, and perseverance, and the sheer knowledge which is an essential of being educated, will decline. These are genuine virtues and an education which does not feature them is faulty.

Society is right to expect that importance will be attached to these virtues in all schools. Children need them and need knowledge, if they are to gain satisfaction from their education. What we repudiate is the view that they were automatically fostered by the old kind of elementary education. Patently they were not, for enormous numbers of the products of that education do not possess them. Still more we repudiate the fear that the modern primary approach leads to their neglect. On the contrary it can and, when properly understood, does lay a much firmer foundation for their development, and it is more in the interests of the children. But those interests are complex. Children need to be themselves, to live with other children and with grown-ups, to learn from their environment, to enjoy the present, to get ready for the future, to create and to love, to learn to face adversity, to behave responsibly, in a word, to be human beings. Decisions about the influences and situations that ought to be contrived to these ends must be left to individual schools, teachers, and parents. What must be ensured is that the decisions taken in schools spring from the best available knowledge and are not simply dictated by habit or convention.

IMPORTANCE OF PLAY

Play is the central activity in all nursery schools and in many infant schools. This sometimes leads to accusations that children are wasting their time in school: they should be "working." But this distinction between work and play is false, possibly throughout life, certainly in the primary school. Its essence lies in past notions of what is done in school hours (work) and what is done out of school (play). We know now that play—in the sense of "messing about," either with material objects or with other children, and of creating fantasies—is vital to children's learning and therefore vital in school. Adults who criticize teachers for allowing children to play are unaware that play is the principal means of learning in early childhood. It is the way through which children reconcile their inner lives with external reality. In play, children gradually develop concepts of causal relationships, the power to discriminate, to make judgments, to analyze and synthesize, to imagine, and to formulate. Children become absorbed in their play, and the satisfaction of bringing it to a satisfactory conclusion fixes habits of concentration which can be transferred to other learning.

From infancy, children investigate the material world. Their interest is not wholly scientific but arises from a desire to control or use the things about them. Pleasure in "being a cause" seems to permeate children's earliest contact with materials. To destroy and construct involves learning the properties of things, and in this way children can build up concepts of weight, height, size, volume, and texture.

Primitive materials such as sand, water, clay, and wood attract young children and evoke concentration and inventiveness. Children are also stimulated by natural or manufactured materials of many shapes, colors, and textures. Their imagination seizes on particular facets of objects and leads them to invent as well as to create. All kinds of causal connections are discovered, illustrated, and used. Children also use objects as symbols for things, feelings, and experiences for which they may lack words. A small girl may use a piece of material in slightly different ways to make herself into a bride, a queen, or a nurse. When teachers enter into the play activity of children, they can help by watching the connections and relationships which children are making and by introducing, almost incidentally, the words for the concepts and feelings that are being expressed. Some symbolism is unconscious and may be the means by which children come to terms with actions or thoughts which are not acceptable to adults or are too frightening for the children themselves. In play are the roots of drama, expressive movement, and art.

In this way, too, children learn to understand other people. The earliest play of this kind probably emerges from play with materials. A child playing with a toy airplane can be seen to take the role of both the airplane and the pilot, apparently simultaneously. All the important people of his world figure in this play: he imitates, he becomes, he symbolizes. He works off aggression or compensates himself for lack of love by "being" one or other of the people who impinge on his life. By acting as he conceives they do, he tries to understand them. Since children tend to have inflexible roles thrust on them by adults, they need opportunities to explore different roles and to make a freer choice of their own. Early exploration of the actions, motives, and feelings of themselves and of others is likely to be an important factor in the ability to form right relationships, which in its turn seems to be a crucial element in mental health. The difficulties of blind and deaf children whose play is restricted show how much play enriches the lives of ordinary children. Adults can help children in this form of play, and in their social development, by references to the thoughts, feelings, and needs of other people. Through stories told to them, children enter into different ways of behaving and of looking at the world and play new parts.

Just as adults relive experience in thought or words, so children play over and over the important happenings of their lives. The repetition is usually selective. Children who reenact a painful scene repeatedly are not doing it to preserve the pain but to make it bearable and understandable. They incorporate those parts of the difficult situation which are endurable and add others as their courage and confidence grow. This is one of the ways in which they bring under control the feelings of frustration which must be experienced by those who are dependent on the will and love of adults. This kind of play can preserve self-esteem by reducing unpleasant experiences to size and reinforce confidence by dwelling on success.

Much of children's play is "cultural" play as opposed to the "natural" play of animals which mainly practices physical and survival skills. It often needs adult participation so that cultural facts and their significance can be communicated to children. The introduction into the classroom of objects for hospital play provides opportunities for coming to terms with one of the most common fears. Similarly the arrival of a new baby in the family, the death of someone important to the child, the invention of space rockets or new weapons may all call for the provision of materials for dramatic play which will help children to give expression to their feelings as a preliminary to understanding and controlling them. Sensitivity and observation are called for rather than intervention from the teacher. The knowledge of children gained from "active" observation is invaluable to teachers. It gives common ground for conversation and exchange of ideas which is among the most important duties of teachers to initiate and foster.

A child's play at any given moment contains many elements. The layers of meaning may include a highly conscious organization of the environment, exploration of physical and social relationships, and an expression of the deepest levels of fantasy. Wide ranging and satisfying play is a means of learning, a powerful stimulus to learning, and a way to free learning from distortion by the emotions. Several writers have recently emphasized the importance of a period of play and exploration in new learning as, for example, in mathematics and science. Adults as well as children approach new learning in this way.

THE CHILD AS AGENT OF HIS OWN LEARNING

The child is the agent in his own learning. This was the message of the often quoted comment from the 1931 Report, *The Hadow Report: A Report of the Consultative Committee on the Primary School* (London: Her Majesty's Stationary Office, 1931): "The curriculum is to be thought of in terms of activity and experience rather than of knowledge to be acquired and facts to be stored." Read in isolation, the passage has sometimes been taken to imply that children could not learn from imaginative experience and that activity and experience did not lead to the acquisition of knowledge. The context makes it plain that the actual implication is almost the opposite of this. It is that activity and experience, both physical and mental, are often the best means of gaining knowledge and acquiring facts. This is more generally recognized today but still needs to be said. We certainly would not wish to undervalue knowledge and facts, but facts are best retained when they are used and understood, when right attitudes to learning are created, when children learn to learn. Instruction in many primary schools continues to bewilder children because it outruns their experience. Even in infant schools, where innovation has gone furthest, time is sometimes wasted in teaching written "sums" before children are able to understand what they are doing.

The intense interest shown by young children in the world about them, their powers of concentration on whatever is occupying their attention or serving their immediate purposes, are apparent to both teachers and parents. Skills of reading and writing or the techniques used in art and craft can best be taught when the need for them is evident to children. A child who has no immediate incentive for learning to read is unlikely to succeed because of warnings about the disadvantages of illiteracy in adult life. There is, therefore, good reason for allowing young children to choose within a carefully prepared environment in which choices and interest are supported by their teachers, who will have in mind the potentialities for further learning. Piaget's observations support the belief that children have a natural urge to explore and discover, that they find pleasure in satisfying it, and that it is therefore self-perpetuating. When children are learning new patterns of behavior or new concepts, they tend both to practice them spontaneously and to seek out relevant experience, as can be seen from the way they acquire skills in movement. It takes much longer than teachers have previously realized for children to master through experience new concepts or new levels of complex concepts. When understanding has been achieved, consolidation should follow. At this stage children profit from various types of practice devised by their teachers and from direct instruction.

Children will, of course, vary in the degree of interest that they show, and their urge to learn will be strengthened or weakened by the attitudes of parents, teachers, and others with whom they identify themselves. Apathy may result when parents show no interest, clamp down on children's curiosity and enterprise, tell them constantly not to touch, and do not answer their questions. Children can also learn to be passive from a teacher who allows them little scope in managing their own affairs and in learning. A teacher who relies only on instruction, who forestalls children's questions, or who answers them too quickly, instead of asking the further questions which will set children on the way to their own solution, will disincline children to learn (John Holt, *How Children Fail.* New York: Pitman, 1964). A new teacher with time and patience can usually help children who have learned from their teachers to be too dependent. Those who have been deprived at home need more than that. Their self-confidence can only be restored by affection, stability, and order. They must have special attention from adults who can discover, by observing their responses, what experiences awaken interest and can seize on them to reinforce the desire to learn.

External incentives, such as marks, stars, and other rewards and punishments, influence children's learning mainly by evoking or representing parents' or teachers' approval. Although children vary temperamentally in their response to rewards and punishments, positive incentives are generally more effective than punishment, and neither is as damaging as neglect. But the children who most need the incentive of good marks are least likely to gain them even when, as in many primary schools, they are given for effort rather than for achievement. In any case, one of the main educational tasks of the primary school is to build on and strengthen children's intrinsic interest in learning and lead them to learn for themselves rather than from fear of disapproval or desire for praise.

Learning is a continuous process from birth. The teacher's task is to provide an environment and opportunities which are sufficiently challenging for children and yet not so difficult as to be outside their reach. There has to be the right mixture of the familiar and the novel, the right match to the stage of learning the child has reached. If the material is too familiar or the learning skills too easy, children will become inattentive and bored. If too great maturity is demanded of them, they fall back on half-remembered formulas and become concerned only to give the reply the teacher wants. Children can think and form concepts, so long as they work at their own level and are not made to feel that they are failures.

Teachers must rely both on their general knowledge of child development and on detailed observation of individual children for matching their demands to children's stages of development. This concept of "readiness" was first applied to reading. It has sometimes been thought of in too negative a way. Children can be led to want to read, provided that they are sufficiently mature. Learning can be undertaken too late as well as too early. Piaget's work can help teachers in diagnosing children's readiness in mathematics and gives some pointers as to how it can be encouraged.

At every stage of learning children need rich and varied materials and situations, though the pace at which they should be introduced may vary according to the children. If children are limited in materials, they tend to solve problems in isolation and fail to see their relevance to other similar situations. This stands out particularly clearly in young children's learning of mathematics. Similarly, children need to accumulate much experience of human behavior before they can develop moral concepts. If teachers or parents are inconsistent in their attitudes or contradict by their behavior what they preach, it becomes difficult for children to develop stable and mature concepts. Verbal explanation, in advance of understanding based on experience, may be an obstacle to learning, and children's knowledge of the right words may conceal from teachers their lack of understanding. Yet it is inevitable that children will pick up words which outstrip their understanding. Discussion with other children and with adults is one of the principal ways in which children check their concepts against those of others and build up an objective view of reality. There is every justification for the conversation which is a characteristic feature of the contemporary primary school. One of the most important responsibilities of teachers is to help children to see order and pattern in experience and to extend their ideas by analogies and by the provision of suitable vocabulary. Rigid division of the curriculum into subjects tends to interrupt children's trains of thought and of interest and to hinder them from realizing the common elements in problem-solving. These are among the many reasons why some work, at least, should cut across subject divisions at all stages in the primary school.

IMPLICATIONS FOR THE CURRICULUM AND SCHEDULE

These beliefs about how children learn have practical implications for the timetable and the curriculum. One idea, now widespread, is embodied in the expression "free day," and another, associated with it, is the "integrated curriculum." The strongest influence making for the free day has been the conviction of some teachers and other educationalists that it is through play that young children learn. Nursery schools began by devoting half an hour to free play. This is still done by many kindergartens which we visited abroad. Now the whole day is spent on various forms of play, though groups of children may break away to enjoy stories or music with an adult. Infant schools usually give at least an hour a day to play, though it may be called by many different names. If teachers encourage overlap between what is done in periods of self-chosen activity and in the times allocated, for example, to reading and to writing, a good learning situation will probably result. Children who are not yet ready to read can go on playing and building up vocabulary while other children are reading. Play can lead naturally to reading and writing associated with it. Children do not flit from activity to activity in their anxiety to make use of materials not available at other times of the day. Some infant schools are now confident enough in the value of self-chosen activity to give the whole day to it, except for times which are used for stories, poetry, movement, and music—and even these may be voluntary, particularly for the younger children. The tendency is spreading in junior schools. Children may plan when to do work assigned to them and also have time in which to follow personal or group interests of their own choice. In a few infant and junior schools the day is still divided into a succession of short periods. In the great majority, we are glad to say, there are longer periods and these can be adjusted at the teacher's discretion.

These changes represent a revolution from the type of timetable implied by the forms completed by schools for local education authorities until quite recently. Heads (principals) were expected to show exactly what each class was doing during every minute of the week and to provide a summary showing the total number of minutes to be spent on each subject. In extreme cases, the curriculum was divided into spelling, dictation, grammar, exercises, composition, recitation, reading, handwriting, tables, and mental arithmetic. It is obvious that this arrangement was not suited to what was known of the nature of children, of the classification of subject matter, or of the art of teaching. Children's interest varies in length according to personality, age, and circumstances, and it is folly either to interrupt it when it is intense or to flog it when it has declined. The teacher can best judge when to make a

147

change, and the moment of change may not be the same for each child in the class. In many schools, as we have said, children plan much of their work. Yet the teacher must constantly ensure a balance within the day or week both for the class and for individuals. He must see that time is profitably spent and give guidance on its use. In the last resort, the teacher's relationship with his pupils, his openness to their suggestions and their trust in him, are far more important than the nominal degree of freedom in the timetable.

The extent to which subject matter ought to be classified and the headings under which the classification is made will vary with the age of the children, with the demands made by the structure of the subject matter being studied, and with the circumstances of the school. Any practice which predetermines the pattern and imposes it upon all is to be condemned. Some teachers find it helpful in maintaining a balance in individual and class work to think in terms of broad areas of the curriculum such as language, science and mathematics, environmental study, and the expressive arts. No pattern can be perfect, since many subjects fall into one category or another according to the aspect which is being studied. For young children, the broadest of divisions is suitable. For children from nine to twelve, more subject divisions can be expected, though experience in secondary schools has shown that teaching of rigidly defined subjects, often by specialist teachers, is far from suitable for the oldest children who will be in the middle schools. This is one of our reasons for suggesting a change in the age of transfer to secondary education.

There is little place for the type of scheme which sets down exactly what ground should be covered and what skill should be acquired by each class in the school. Yet to put nothing in its place may be to leave some teachers prisoners of tradition and to make difficulties for newcomers to a staff who are left to pick up, little by little, the ethos of a school. The best solution seems to be to provide brief schemes for the school as a whole: outlines of aims in various areas of the curriculum, the sequence of development which can be expected in children, and the methods through which work can be soundly based and progress accelerated. It is also useful to have a record of experiences, topics, books, poems, and music which have been found to succeed with children of different ages, and for attention to be drawn to notable experimental work. In good schools, schemes are often subject to a process of accretion which may make them so long that few teachers have time to read them. It is better for them to be sifted and revised, for matter to be dropped as well as added. Individual members of staff, with such help as the head and others can give, will need to plan in more detail the work of their particular classes. Often it will develop in an unexpected direction. A brief report on the topics, literature, and so forth which have absorbed children during the course of the year will be necessary for teachers who take them later in their school career.

WAYS OF INTEGRATING THE CURRICULUM

The idea of flexibility has found expression in a number of practices, all of them designed to make good use of the interest and curiosity of children, to minimize the notion of subject matter being rigidly compartmental, and to allow the teacher to adopt a consultative, guiding, stimulating role rather than a purely didactic one. The oldest of these methods is the "project." Some topic, such as "transport," is chosen, ideally by the children but frequently by the teacher. The topic cuts across the boundaries of subjects and is treated as its nature requires without reference to subjects as such. At its best the method leads to the use of books of reference, to individual work, and to active participation in learning. Unfortunately, there is no

149

guarantee of this, and the appearance of textbooks of projects, which achieved at one time considerable popularity, is proof of how completely a good idea can be misunderstood.

A variation on the project, originally associated with the infant school but often better suited to older children, is "the center of interest." It begins with a topic which is of such inherent interest and variety as to make it possible and reasonable to make much of the work of the class revolve round it for a period of a week, a month, a term, or even longer. Experience has shown that it is artificial to try to link most of the work of a class to one center of interest. It has become more common to have several interests—"topic" is now the usual word—going at once. Much of the work may be individual, falling under broad subject headings. One topic for the time being can involve both group and class interest, and may splinter off into all kinds of individual work.

When a class of seven-year-olds notice the birds that come to the bird table outside the classroom window, they may decide, after discussion with their teacher, to make their own aviary. They will set to with a will and paint the birds in flight, make models of them in clay or papier-mâché, write stories and poems about them, and look up reference books to find out more about their habits. Children are not assimilating inert ideas but are wholly involved in thinking, feeling, and doing. The slow and the bright share a common experience, and each takes from it what he can at his own level. There is no attempt to put reading and writing into separate compartments; both serve a wider purpose, and artificial barriers do not fragment the learning experience.

A top junior class became interested in the problem of measuring the area of an awkwardly shaped field at the back of the school. The problem stimulated much learning about surveying and triangles. From surveying, interest passed to navigation; for the more difficult aspects of the work, cooperation between members of staff as well as pupils was needed. For one boy, the work on navigation took the form of a story of encounters of pirate ships and men-of-war and involved a great deal of calculation, history, geography, and English. Integration is not only a question of allowing time for interests which do not fit under subject headings; it is as much a matter of seeing the different dimensions of subject work and of using the forms of observation and communication which are most suitable to a given sequence of learning.

Another effective way of integrating the curriculum is to relate it through the use of the environment to the boundless curiosity which children have about the world about them. When teachers talk about firsthand experience, what they often have in mind is the exploration of the physical environment of the school, though the expression, of course, includes other kinds of experiences as well. Whereas once the teacher brought autumn leaves into the classroom and talked about the seasons and their characteristics, now he will take the children out to see for themselves. Rural schools can be overwhelmed by the variety of material on their doorsteps. Crops and pastures, wild flowers and weeds, farm animals, wild creatures of every kind, roads and footpaths, verges (road shoulders), hedges, ditches, streams, woods, the weather, the season, the stars, all provide starting points for curiosity, discussion, observation, recording, and inquiry at every level from that of the five-year-old to that of the twelve-year-old and beyond. Much of this material is also available to the newer urban schools, though their sites are often laid out too formally to be suitable for children's play or for interesting studies. The most difficult problem of all is not so much that of the older urban school, despite its often restricted site, as that of the school on a large housing estate. But the weather and the stars are available to all;

so are the occupations of fathers which offer a way of enlisting cooperation and interest in their children's education as well as an approach to local industry.

Teachers in town schools can make use of railways and other transport systems, the local shops, and factories, all of which can provide suitable material. Building sites are almost ubiquitous and can provide an approach to geography, mathematics, and science. We have heard of children doing "traffic counts," discovering from shopkeepers the source of their goods, and even, in one case, exploring unofficially the sewage system of their area. Museums geared to children's interests may also be within reach and are becoming ready to let children handle as well as look, and to lend to schools some of the surplus stock which is otherwise often stored away in basements. It may be well to look a little at this approach as it can work out in a favorable environment. A group of H.M.I.s (inspectors) working in a division in which some particularly good work is to be found write as follows:

The newer methods start with the direct impact of the environment on the child and the child's individual response to it. The results are unpredictable but extremely worthwhile. The teacher has to be prepared to follow up the personal interests of the children who, either singly or in groups, follow divergent paths of discovery. Books of reference, maps, inquiries of local offiicials, museums, archives, elderly residents in the area are all called upon to give the information needed to complete the picture that the child is seeking to construct. When this enthusiasm is unleashed in a class, the timetable may even be dispensed with, as the resulting occupations may easily cover mathematics, geology, astronomy, history, navigation, religious instruction, literature, art, and craft. The teacher needs perception to appreciate the value that can be gained from this method of working, and he needs also energy to keep up with the children's demands.

Another possibility is to take children out of their own environment into a contrasting one, either for the day or for a longer period. This, of course, applies as much to rural children visiting towns as to urban children visiting the countryside. Such visits, carefully prepared for and not just sight-seeing, are generally used as the culmination of an interest or interests. They would often serve better as starting points. For day visits, when the school situation makes it possible, those places are best which are near enough for children to visit and to revisit, individually, in groups, or as a class when new questions arise. There is then a strong incentive for them to look closely at the objects which have made a further visit necessary.

In one northern city a school, well situated in a park on the outskirts of the city, is being used for a fortnight at a time by children from the central slum areas. The school has a small resident staff and is well equipped. Since the visiting children's own teachers accompany them, they can be taught in small groups of fifteen. During the summer months the school day is extended into the evening so that the children, who are conveyed by buses, can gain the maximum from their experiences.

Local education authorities can help schools, as some indeed do, by providing hutted camps and other residential centers which do much for children socially as well as educationally. Useful experiments have also been tried in linking country and urban schools and arranging for exchange visits. Expeditions too far afield are to be avoided, as they are generally speaking pure sight-seeing tours. We have considerable doubts about overseas expeditions for primary school children.

A third possibility, which is open to all schools, is to make the school environment itself as rich as possible. Nearly all children are interested in living forms, whether they be animal or plants. Some acquaintance with them is an essential part of being educated. To care for living creatures offers an emotional outlet to some children and demands discipline from all. However rich the locality, emphasis must always be put on the school itself, which is an environment contrived for children's learning.

A word which has fairly recently come into use in educational circles is "discovery." It includes many of the ideas so far discussed and is a useful shorthand description. It has the disadvantage of comprehensiveness that it can be loosely interpreted and misunderstood. (We have more to say about the value of discovery in the section on science.) The sense of personal discovery influences the intensity of a child's experience, the vividness of his memory, and the probability of effective transfer of learning. At the same time, it is true that trivial ideas and inefficient methods may be "discovered." Furthermore, time does not allow children to find their way by discovery to all that they have to learn. In this matter, as in all education, the teacher is responsible for encouraging children in inquiries which lead to discovery and for asking leading questions.

Free and sometimes indiscriminate use of words such as "discovery" has led some critics to the view that English primary education needs to be more firmly based on closely argued educational theory. Nevertheless great advances appear to have been made without such theory, and research has still a long way to go before it can make a marked contribution. At many points even so fruitful an approach as that of Piaget needs further verification. What is immediately needed is that teachers should bring to bear on their day-to-day problems astringent intellectual scrutiny. Yet all good teachers must work intuitively and be sensitive to the emotive and imaginative needs of their children. Teaching is an art and, as long as that with all its implications is firmly grasped, it will not be harmed by intellectual stiffening.

ON PREPARING THE TEACHER: A LESSON FROM LOUGHBOROUGH

by Charles H. Rathbone

With the arrival of the Plowden Report came a host of rumors about "informal" infant classrooms, "integrated day" scheduling, widespread use of vertical or "family" grouping. Many Americans were led to ask about the effects of these innovations, not only on children's learning in schools but on curriculum reform, school organization, teacher training, and the like. It was with curiosity, therefore, that I journeyed to England in the spring of 1968; in particular I wanted to test the rumors about teacher education against the hard reality.

My trip was divided into three quite distinct parts. I visited a number of infant and junior schools in Leicestershire, Oxfordshire, Bristol, and London. Then, too, I had a number of personal interviews with representatives of the National Froebel Foundation, Goldsmiths' Curriculum Laboratory, the Nuffield Maths Project, the National Foundation for Educational Research, the Froebel Institute, and the Department of Child Development at the University of London's Institute of Education. But in terms of teacher education, the most remarkable experience I had was a personal one associated with the third phase of my trip. A description of that phase as well as some reflections on it provide the substance of the following report. It is offered in the hope that teacher educators as well as practicing teachers might come to recognize the benefits of viewing both teaching and learning from the perspective informally outlined here.

THE IN-SERVICE TRAINING COURSE

In April, 1968, I attended an in-service training course organized by the Leicestershire Education Department Advisory Section at the Loughborough University of Technology. It lasted a week, from Wednesday through Wednesday. Then in its third year, the course was again oversubscribed. Of those there, the majority by far were full-time, practicing primary school teachers, and half of them were men. In addition, there were a half-dozen primary heads and perhaps a dozen secondary school teachers as well as a few people from outside the County schools, such as myself and a lady from the training college. Total enrollment neared eighty; occasionally there were one-day visitors.

Although the course was located in Loughborough in central England, near Nottingham, there was no official affiliation with the university, nor was there credit nor any monetary compensation. In fact, participants were accountable to no one but themselves; no advancement, tenure, or grades depended on their performance. Although the Advisory section in part subsidized the tuition, each teacher was asked to pay a registration fee out of pocket. Moreover, all voluntarily forfeited nearly half their Easter holiday.

The proportion of staff to participants was amazingly high. The Advisory must have provided ten or twelve people, and added to that nucleus were perhaps another dozen staff members from outside the County—some American imports, some Nuffield, Froebel, and Goldsmiths' curriculum-making people, plus some experienced teachers who were headed toward adviserships elsewhere or toward becoming members of Her Majesty's Inspectorate. In any case, the over-all ratio approximated better than four students to each staff member.

The overt organization of the course was minimal. There were five or six workshop rooms, which opened after breakfast each day and remained open until nine or ten at night. Meals were scheduled, as was a forty-minute tea break and mid-afternoon coffee. In addition there were two barrooms on the premises—one a permanent facility for the university students, the other a makeshift affair created especially for us and located beneath our dining hall. The large blocks of scheduled but undirected time proved unexpectedly important as the week progressed, for they not only provided opportunity to relax and meditate but also fostered serious, professional shoptalk.

From time to time special activities were made available. These included a couple of lectures, three or four films, some field trips, and as many special meetings as anyone chose to call. If it seemed desirable to spend a concentrated hour on one particular phase of math or music, a notice would go up announcing the session (always voluntary). Usually these meetings were called by a staff person (though often at the urging of a group of us); occasionally a participant would call his own. When a special interest was voiced, the course responded.

In the workshop area there was a room for art and a room for natural science, one for mathematics, one for English, one for physical science, and one for music. But these general labels inadequately describe what the rooms were really like, for both within the rooms and among them was a wide variety of both materials available and uses to which they might be put. Take for example the so-called "art" room. There were paints—poster paints, oils, watercolors, and any mixture anyone cared to attempt—and there was an assortment of brushes. There were car-

157

pentry tools and sculpturing tools and tiny curved knives for cutting linoleum, wire cutters and wire, tin and tin cans, plaster, Plasticine, crayons, and rope. There was wool and thread, egg crates and cardboard cartons, little sticks and tongue depressors, balsa wood and glue, tissue paper and poster paper, cardboard and string, and books on print-making, paper-folding, knot-tying and embroidery. Moving among all these inanimate resources were a number of highly skilled and ready-to-help peers as well as some-one called the art teacher.

In sum, the room was crammed with opportunities, stuffed with stuff to do. But that was just the first day; thereafter there was more, dragged in by those of us who were using the room. I myself introduced a couple of corks, swiped from the room next door where people were studying the movement of bubbles as they passed through various densities of liquid in stoppered tubes. I also personally brought in (needing a model to sketch from as I prepared my lino block) a book on bugs from the natural science room and some white shiny cardboard (also snitched from the bug room), which I needed for mounting the poems I had written in the "English" room earlier that morning.

It was an active, changing environment, and we were often actively instrumental in changing it to suit our individual needs. No constraints were placed on our mobility, nor was there pressure to "cover" any particular subject area. After all, we were teachers and we were adult; we had well-developed preferences and motives of our own. What this special world allowed was a self-multiplying set of options, so that my introduction of one new material might directly affect the number of options available to someone nearby.

Staff "teachers" were present, of course, but they were quiet and unobtrusive—easy to find but not much noticed otherwise. They lived among us, ate at no special table, and were generally indistinguishable from participants; if they gathered together for special staff meetings, they did so inconspicuously. When called on, they materialized; when not, they somehow faded into the background, into the woodwork, into their own work. Although the staff on many occasions did instigate and guide, it was usually *after* the initial contact had been made by one of us; their role seemed to demand considerably more *reaction* than *action*. The traditional class lesson, with the teacher addressing large groups on a topic of his choice, was rare.

There were, nonetheless, some group activities, though even these were unregimented. Take the "P.E. to Music" program, for example. Here we had a visiting instructor, a man who was only with the course for a couple of days. Up went a sign-up sheet, and the next morning we duly assembled, in sneakers, in the gymnasium. There was the instructor, armed with tapes and an obvious agenda. His way of operating within the constraints—his limited time in Loughborough, our limited endurance—was to plan carefully every phase of the morning's activity. So put us through our paces he did. As a group we were set a sequence of obviously ordered exercises, yet within those set assignments there remained considerable opportunity to individualize both the requirements and the solution. For example, he asked us to move about the gymnasium floor developing a "series of punches." The music was slow waltz time. To this task there was no obviously "right" response; in our own ways we were all "right" from the moment we began. Interpretation might be questioned but not "correctness." Yet we improved—we grew—and our growth during the morning was perceptible. His informed commentary was especially helpful in enabling us to enlarge our vocabulary of response. By pointing out how someone was "following through" on his punch, or how someone else was using an uppercut, or an elbow, or punching backward, he kept us in touch with a constantly increasing number of options, many of which we assimilated into our own patterns.

However personal and idiosyncratic that P.E. learning may have been, it was thoroughly and from the start bound by the intent of the instructor and his lesson. This was not always so; sometimes the ultimate content of a "class" was only tangentially related to any originally intended curriculum. The instructors tolerated unanticipated shifts in the interests of the participants; their flexibility in this regard made a number of unexpected curricula possible.

For instance, one day a notice appeared advertising a field trip, organized by the natural science staff man. The following morning a number of participants went out to visit a nearby stream. They returned bearing literally hundreds of living creatures, which they proceeded to identify and classify, transplant, and encapsulate. But it was from an apparently peripheral incident that the most exciting study evolved. On the way to the stream, the bus had passed a field where there were some badger holes. No one on the bus had ever seen a badger, it seemed, and as the conversation continued, interest mounted. Someone recalled hearing of a local gentleman reputed to be knowledgeable on these elusive, nocturnal animals. A phone call followed; a lecture was arranged. It turned out the man was one of the foremost badger experts in all Europe; his talk and excellent slides were enthusiastically received, especially those parts concerned with baiting—that is, with the techniques of luring the animal from his lair so that he may be seen and studied. Needless to say, for the next three or four afternoons, just at dusk, badgerbaiting parties went forth into the surrounding countryside, armed with field glasses and ripe, uncooked ham

This episode typifies the experience of "instant curriculum"—that organic evolution of a "subject" or a "topic" around which many people could loosely group. It was a context that developed almost by itself; public expression of personal interest, encouraged by other voices and fed by increased understanding and more sophisticated questioning, produced on the spot a topical and relevant curriculum, one that might have led on to the economics of shaving brushes, or the cellular chemistry of night vision, or whatever. The point is, these "subjects" *led from* earlier, more naive, and less discipline-bound questions. The movement could not have been in the opposite direction, and any teacher who might have tried suckering these students into a lesson on optics by beginning with badgers, owls, and moles, would have been hooted down. The lesson of the badger incident is that the teacher, given— and giving—this context of freedom, cannot predetermine what will be learned. He can be prepared for numerous eventualities, he can, on the basis of past performance and enthusiasm, predict the probabilities, but never will he be able, with certainty, to say what will happen next.

This, then, describes the course—at least from a participant's view. Its elements were comparatively uncomplicated and unrevolutionary: a competent staff, well equipped with materials and unfettered by rigidity of curriculum or schedule; a suitable location and sufficient time to get something started; a group of talented, self-selected participants.

Treated as though we had both the competence and the right to make important decisions about our own learning, we were let "do our own thing," unrestricted by teacher expectations or by deference to an obligatory corpus of knowledge declared by some higher authority to be indispensable. Learning at every turn was individualized; flexibility the watchword. In the end I had little doubt that those responsible for the course had deliberately attempted to construct precisely the environment that would provide, for the teachers, a model of what their own classrooms might be like. It was the structure of the course, then, that offered the most systematic instruction—in Loughborough the medium was indeed the message.

THOUGHTS ON STAFF, MATERIALS, AND SELF

Yet the quality of the experience differed from that of an ordinary teachers' workshop; the quality of the Loughborough experience was truly different, and no simple enumeration of its components can adequately account for that uniqueness. When I left Loughborough, I was still looking for a missing component; now I think the answer lies instead somewhere *between* the components. For, hidden among the overt offerings, was a context in which each of us was able to find opportunity for significant personal growth.

I asked myself one day exactly what it was I had learned at Loughborough. The answer turned out to be a very personal "who am I" kind of response. For—aside from the bits and snatches of biology and history I had picked up during my week there—the most meaningful insight concerned myself, specifically myself as a student in a learning situation.

The relation of myself to the staff, of myself to the materials, and of myself to myself-as-learner, these three, generalized to the course as a whole, are what mattered most. The realization of the significance of these elements —not for myself alone but for teachers at every stage of development—and the realization that the quality of each of these relationships could be improved upon within the framework of a workshop like this—these were the insights that so expanded the potential of the entire enterprise for me.

An incident occurred a week or so after I left Loughborough that helped me to put my finger on a significant factor in any student-teacher relationship—how students perceive the teacher's role. One day, visiting an infant class in Bristol, I was asked point-blank by a tiny miss whose name I have forgotten, "Please, sir, would you give me butterfly?" I blanched a bit, asked the question to be repeated a couple of times, and finally heard, "Would you give me *butterfly?*"—the spelling of the word "butterfly" for her self-made speller, the kind that all the children carry with them when they're writing. Herein (shades of Sylvia Ashton-Warner) she kept the words *she* wanted to learn, and already—she couldn't have been much more than five—she had learned to make maximum use of available resources, even when those resources seemed slightly hard of hearing or a bit stupid or foreign, like this American visitor.

Often at Loughborough, old assumptions about teachers prevented me from taking advantage of the available resources with similar naiveté. Just as I had mistakenly expected the little girl to be using spelling as a means of initiating a conversation ultimately aimed at monopolizing my attention (which was not the case at all; once she had the word, off she went—polite and matter-of-fact), so I found myself shy or embarrassed, resentful, or anxious in my relationships with staff instructors. "What would they think of me, asking such a dumb question?" "Hadn't I already used up more than my share of time?" These unvoiced questions placed enormous constraints on my freedom to learn.

What Loughborough offered was an opportunity for me to witness, for the first time really, how an outmoded concept of student role operated within myself. By presenting an environment particularly conducive to an alternative set of relationships between student and teacher, it revealed the true nature of the model I brought with me to the course.

In a like manner I found myself having difficulty with

certain materials—not because my fingers fumbled or because I was stupid but because of a fundamental inability to release myself to the learning situation. I am reminded of the day in the science room when I faced the batteries and bulbs. Nothing there could free me from the fetters of some long-forgotten, authority-directed "truth" about those silly batteries; nothing I was able to do could release me from my own dim past when many years ago I had "learned" electricity. Try as I might, I was unable to approach those materials in the unassuming, unpresuming, honest ignorance that was required for me to learn from them. Instead, I racked my brain to remember the rules I had once committed to memory—the rules I suspect were learned indirectly, from a text or a teacher or a lab partner's notebook.

At Loughborough I was constantly confronting neutral material—classroom stuff that displayed no attitude whatsoever toward me. Yet time and time again I found myself unable to accept what was there; either I would seek some prepackaged "lesson" or I would look to the teacher for clues on how I was "supposed" to define and solve some predetermined "problem." The difficulty lay in feeling free to ask my *own* questions, yet this is precisely the possibility the Loughborough experience made me aware of.

My hesitancy with materials and the artificiality of my relationship to my instructors contributed to the image I had of myself as a learner in the Loughborough situation. As I think back over the workshops, I sense I was good in the English room, poor at maths, experienced in dabbling with paints, and inept at movement or dance. Thus at times I was among the more competent, at others a rank novice who might profitably accept aid from a more experienced peer. The effect of seeing myself this way made me avoid the negative assumption-making a singular point of view so often brings. Assessing my skills *in context* provided a sliding scale of self-esteem, many points of view from which to view myself. Neither athletic competence nor academic success, as in my own school days, was permitted to dominate. Nor was any other single measurement.

Mixed, vertical grouping similarly discouraged any simple and inflexible view of how I thought the teacher was seeing me. I knew, for instance, that what the art teacher offered me as I was painting was quite different from what she offered when I was fumbling with the linoleum-cutting tools. Likewise I knew the counsel she offered to competent craftsmen contrasted sharply with her advice to novices. I could see that she was constrained at each intervention to take into account the particular context of each student's work, and in my case that differed radically as I moved from task to task.

Success should be easy to acknowledge. When you find out how to solve a math puzzle, it's just natural you want to explain the solution to someone else; or, after you have worked a full hour on a drawing and it's finally finished, it seems quite right and even pleasurable to place it on the bulletin board alongside your friend's. At least that's true when you're confident and not too anxious about receiving someone else's approval of your work, when acceptance of yourself as learner comes easily. But when that's not the case, joy vanishes. Consider how I felt when I finished my first linoleum block. As someone else said about *his* attempt in this medium, he hadn't done a lino block for nearly twenty years, and during the interval there had been little progress in either style or accuracy. His 1968 effort reminded him above all else of the work of an eight-year-old.

For me it was horribly difficult to admit being connected with my drab little print; it required real humility before I was prepared to own up and accept, without embarrassment, full responsibility for this thing I had created. To discover where you are in respect to lino blocks and to find that you are still at the eight-year-old level is disconcerting. It means, first, admitting that the work you do is an indication of your competence and a reflection— to some significant extent— of who you are. In the second place, it means an admission that in terms of this particular competency, in respect to this particular part of you, you're a dismal failure.

Becoming aware of where you stand can be humiliating; the process of growing and changing, of suddenly moving away from an earlier position, can be profoundly shocking. I remember, walking back from lunch to the general workshop area one day, encountering a young deputy head who had spent the morning at a dancing workshop. When I inquired how it had gone, his answer startled me. "Disturbing," he replied in far more seriousness than I had asked, "deeply, emotionally disturbing." For several minutes we considered his reaction, and I continued to ponder its meaning as the week went on. He had been shaken by an experience that had required more of him than he considered available. An opportunity had arisen to test his resources; he had accepted, and in accepting the challenge, he had in fact stretched those resources— or at least he had stretched *his own estimation* of their limits. Now he knew he was somehow different. Although I'm sure he would have been hard-pressed to define the precise nature of the change, it certainly had occurred, and he was very nearly frightened. Successful learning does mean change, including change in one's own estimation of oneself. To be able to adapt swiftly and without anguish to a new notion of self seems a very necessary prerequisite to continued success in learning.

What I found at Loughborough was a climate, a psychological environment that jarred a number of long-entrenched preconceptions. Whether this climate actually *caused* new insights to occur, I cannot say; what I am sure of is that it precluded the automatic reinforcement of a number of old attitudes. In respect to at least three relationships—of myself to the materials, myself to teacher-figures, myself to my own image of myself as a learner—I came to see myself more clearly, and that insight into what *already* existed made new changes possible. So in the end the lesson I took from Loughborough was a lesson about learning, a lesson of how a particular context for growth can precipitate confrontation with the debilitating constraints imposed by one's own psyche, a lesson, finally, about the education of teachers, but a lesson, first, about myself.

A CLASSROOM FOR YOUNG CHILDREN: APPROXIMATION NO. I

by Allan Leitman and Edith H. E. Churchill

The task of outfitting a classroom forces the teacher to find a satisfactory balance between theoretical ideal and practical reality. Here, two early members of the Elementary Science Study staff report on their initial approximation of the ideal they sought for a Head Start classroom in 1965.

This classroom[1] is our answer to a question that arose when we were asked to set up a model Head Start class-

---

[1]This particular room is the result of the cooperative effort of our own staff and the following Wheelock College seniors: Susan Bright, Nancy Clarke, Martha Dole, Jane Dexter, Susan Gardner, Sarah Martin, Marietta Pillsbury, Janne Pontius, Ruth Tilghman, Elizabeth Walker, and Gloria Williams. As the room was developed, we consulted Frances Hawkins of Boulder, Colorado; Ilse Mattick of Boston University and Head Start; Leonard Sealey of Leicester, England; Elizabeth Ann Liddle, Henry Haskell, Lynn Gehri, and Alice Kelliher, all of Wheelock College. In final determinations we based our decisions upon experiences gathered at our work in Jamaica Plain Day Care Center, Boston; Houghton School, Cambridge; Shady Hill School, Cambridge; Hills and Falls Nursery School, Wellesley; the Red Barn Nursery School, Weston; the South End Settlement House and the Dorchester Settlement House (all in Massachusetts).

x

168

room, namely: What can be assembled in a limited time to provide an adequate learning environment for young children? We placed the classroom in an old warehouse so that we could familiarize ourselves with the problems of building such a classroom from the ground up. We used this opportunity to find out just how much it takes in terms of people, money, and materials to do the job in ten days' time. We tried to make the room as attractive and inviting to children as possible, but our emphasis was on material for children's use rather than on furniture. The room was organized to include familiar objects and to provide maximum possibilities for young children to explore materials and to find and solve problems.

Each major activity area for this setting was developed by Wheelock College students. The students were in an experimental program sponsored jointly by Elementary Science Study and Wheelock; it included eleven students and one instructor. The students' program relied most heavily on involvement with children, and there were many field trips to observe other ongoing classrooms. In seminars on methods, problems relating to actual classroom situations and the development of materials for preschool classes were discussed. The Wheelock students selected and organized materials and built many objects for children's work in art, music, woodwork, reading, water play, sand play, science, dress-up, and housekeeping.[2]

An important part of teaching consists of being able to step back and watch children's activities. Through their play, children give clues and signals that thoughtful teach-

---

[2]For a more detailed report about the teacher training program that the students who helped develop this prototype classroom were involved with, see Henry S. Haskell, "Teacher Preparation—A Dynamic, Personalized Approach," *Childhood Education,* March 1966, and Allan Leitman, "The Unified Teaching Experiment," *ESI Quarterly Report,* Spring/Summer 1966, Education Development Center (55 Chapel Street, Newton, Mass. 02160).

FLOOR PLAN

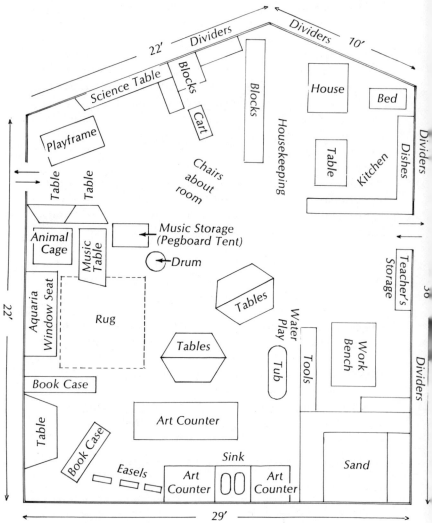

ers can use for planning and decision-making. The room arrangement allows the teacher to be aware of what is happening and allows the child to be aware of the teacher's support without being overwhelmed by her presence. The teacher can move easily to a child who needs her assistance in using materials or in playing with other children. A child can move out of the immediate presence of the teacher when this is what he needs; he can learn to go to adults for help or use their support more indirectly.

The layout of the room makes materials readily available and offers an organization that may be a first experience with an orderly environment for many children. The arrangement of materials in this classroom reflects our conviction that children can *learn* to use these materials responsibly. All the materials are, therefore, located where children can reach them without adult assistance. It may take some time for children coming into this environment to know just what to do with the materials and how to explore and manage them.

We are also well aware that this wide a variety of materials is too overwhelming for the first day of school; so our classroom more nearly represents the situation we hope to achieve after some period of time—perhaps a week or two after school starts but quite possibly much longer. We visualize building up to this total classroom by introducing materials gradually.

For example, our woodworking area has the hammers and saws accessible. Some teachers may prefer not to introduce tools right away. Each teacher will have to make her own decisions on timing and will establish such rules for tool use as her judgment and the temperament of her group of children dictate.

With animals, we anticipate that before the animals appear, children will set up the equipment, prepare the environment, and talk about what is needed to care for animals. When the teacher feels that the children are ready to be responsible for the care of animals, she will introduce them in whatever way seems best. The choice of animals for classroom must be left to the teacher, whether mammals, reptiles, fish, or none.

The work of the class should help children become really involved in their own learning and be successful on their own terms. In this way children achieve a feeling of their power to understand and to change their world.

A NOTE OF CAUTION

We do not believe that this room is finished or that it should be considered as *the* model for Head Start classrooms. It is, at best, a trial setup that will have to be tested under real conditions in order to be proven. We know that some of the items in the original classroom are not the best possible selections, in terms of function as well as price; they merely represent what was at hand at the time. Nor do we insist that these particular materials are the only ones for helping children learn, and we are sure that many teachers, with far less than we have assembled here, will be able to build excellent programs. By assembling this room, we hoped that we might be able to provide a starting point for teachers who are setting up their own rooms. Please remember that our Approximation No. 1 is only to be used as a point of departure. It cannot be used as a shopping list for setting up a classroom or for seeking a budget.

AN INVENTORY
OF CLASSROOM CONTENTS

Storage and Furniture (Approximate total cost, $375.[3])

16 children's chairs
Three 4-shelf storage units
from Sears Roebuck (with
storage boxes)
One 3-shelf storage unit
from Sears Roebuck (with
storage boxes)
8 trapezoidal tables,
homemade
3 student easels, homemade
Pegboard assembly for tools
Pegboard tent for musical
instruments

2 ESS multi-purpose room
dividers
Pegboard hooks
ESS room dividers
20 8" x 8" x 8" cinder blocks
19 6" x 8" x 12" cinder blocks
Planks
ESS tote carts
Wastebasket
Brooms, adult size with
handle cut to child length
Dustpan and brush
Carpet sweeper
First-aid kit

ROOM DIVIDERS

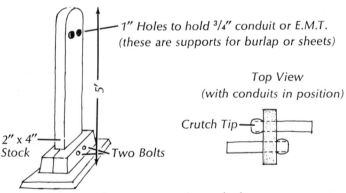

1" Holes to hold ³/₄" conduit or E.M.T.
(these are supports for burlap or sheets)

Top View
(with conduits in position)

Crutch Tip

5'

2" x 4"
Stock   Two Bolts

Using sheets over the supports makes a shadow screen.

---

[3]The total costs for each area are approximate. They indicate what it cost in 1965 to equip this classroom. Specific choices were often dictated by expediency.

EASEL

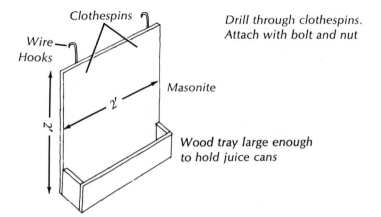

Clothespins

Wire Hooks

Drill through clothespins.
Attach with bolt and nut

Masonite

2'

2'

Wood tray large enough
to hold juice cans

PEGBOARD TENT

Display Board

Divider

Storage

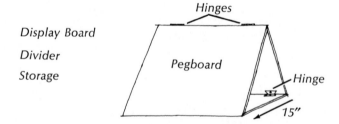

Hinges

Pegboard

Hinge

15"

48" x 36" Sheets of pegboard

Books (Approximate total cost, $100.)

Thirty books were selected to be enjoyed by the children; they included many picture books, favorite stories, and poems to be read to the children. There were also a number of home-made cloth "feely" books with buttons, zippers, shoelaces, and *the like. In addition, seven music books were provided for the teacher's use.*

An old rug and some pillows were placed between the bookcases and the animal area to encourage quieter moments for animal-watching, reading, and music.

Animals and Plants (Approximate total cost, $75.)

ESS gerbil cage
2 gerbils (mated pair)
    from Tumble Brook Farms,
    Inc., Brant Lake, N.Y. 12815,
    and shipped REA Express in
    cagelike wooden box with
    food for a day or two.

Dirt

15-gallon aquarium
Aquarium divider
Goldfish bowl
Aquarium gravel
Refrigerator dishes

Fish net
Floating thermometer

Quart pitcher
Measuring spoons
Baster

Guppies
Polliwogs and frog eggs

Plants (for decoration of
    room as well as for
    aquarium or terrarium)

Other equipment in this
    area included: rug,
    pillows, telephones (on
    loan), Polaroid camera
    and film, and tape recorder.

Toys (Approximate total cost, $50.)

Homemade toys: wooden
    toy trucks, toy train,
    wooden airplanes, toy
    cars, animal and people
    figures

Fisher-Price Creative Blocks
Lego
Blockhead
Slinky
Frame Mosaic
Playskool Parquetry Blocks

Dominoes

Picture dominoes
Giant Lotto
Colorforms
8 wooden puzzles
ESS Attribute Blocks, 2 sets
ESS Pattern Blocks

Curtain rings (to string)
Shoe laces, yarn, elastic cord
Plastic snap beads

Stuffed animals
Hand puppets
Metal toy trucks

175

Blocks and Some Other Building Materials
(Approximate total cost, $230.)

Much of the building equipment listed below is used outside as well as inside.

Hollow Blocks (Half school set from Community Playthings, Rifton, N.Y. 12471)

Unit Blocks (Half school set from Community Playthings)

Set of ESS blocks

ESS Playframe

Tinker Toys (large set)

Assorted springs

Assorted wood turnings

Assorted empty cardboard boxes

Small pulleys

Nuts and bolts

String

Rubber bands

Wheels

Assorted strips of pegboard

Sand (Approximate total cost, $78.)

Many of the items listed below can be used in other areas, particularly outside. Of course sand will also invite adoption of materials from other areas for use here.

39 concrete blocks (8″ x 8″ x 8″ and 30″ x 12″ x 3″)

12′ x 16′ tarplin (government surplus)

3 entrenching tools (government surplus shovels)

Garden shovel

4 rubber mats (at entrance, to wipe feet)

600 lbs. of sand

3 trowels

2 shrub rakes

Watering can

2 plastic pails

Stones (gathered locally)

Driftwood

Sieves

Scoops

Wooden and plastic spoons

Empty soda bottles and sprinkler tops

Empty cans (many different sizes)

Pie plates

Funnels

Large assortment of containers of various sizes and shapes such as the ones used in water play.

176

Water (Approximate total cost, $70.)

Many of the items listed below might also be used in the sand area and outside.

Water sink with high mounted faucet
Til tub and homemade stand
Plastic pails: two, 11-quart size; one, gallon size; one

Lug-a-Jug (5-gallon, collapsible); one collapsible pail
Round plastic dishpan
String mop, with handle cut down to child size

A large collection of plastic bottles, from gallon size to the tiniest, with as many different sizes and shapes as possible, such as liquid detergent bottles, ice-cream containers, plastic ketchup dispensers, etc.

Funnels
Strainers
Scoops
Measuring cups
Plastic beakers
Cigar tubes with stoppers
TV-dinner pans
Straws
Basters
Droppers

Hand pump
Syringes
Vaseline
Sponges
Ethafoam (Dow) expanded polyethylene
Styrofoam balls
Plasticine
Marbles
Short pieces of doweling

'TIL' TUB AND STAND

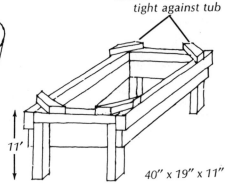

Corner cleats nailed tight against tub

Sears Jumbo Tub

11'

40" x 19" x 11"

Housekeeping (Approximate total cost, $65.)

Many of the items listed below might be used in other areas as well. A large refrigerator carton might well serve as a store one day or a den the next. Here, too, cinder blocks and planks serve for storage, and an old wooden dairy box is an all-purpose chest.

Cinder blocks and planks
Cardboard shelves
Play sink (crate holding 2 square plastic dishpans)
Play stove (cinder blocks supporting plywood top with real stove knobs attached)
Pegboard with hooks to hang scoops, etc.
2 small aprons
Broom, floor mop (adult size with handles cut down to child size)
Scrub brush
Dust pan and brush
Plastic bucket
Sponges
Plastic scouring pad
Dinner plates
Plastic juice pitcher
Adult size forks, spoons, knives (4 of each)
Adult size plastic milk glasses, juice glasses, insulated glasses (4 of each)
Baby bottle
Plastic mixing bowls
Egg beater
Spreaders (2 wooden mixing, 1 icing)
Sifter
Measuring cups, spoons

Cookie cutters
Rolling pins
Metal juice cans
Empty egg cartons
Empty food containers

Wooden milk box to house dress-up clothes
Full-length mirror
Hand mirror
Dress-up clothes: hats, scarves, gloves, pocketbooks, ties, fur stole, shirts, blouses, skirts, dresses, material remnants, scraps of yarn, old shoes, boots, plastic sunglasses, eyeglass frames, shaving brush and empty razor
Buttons, material with buttonholes.

Child's bed, homemade with foam mattress
Small pillow
Crib blanket
Dolls, Negro and white
Doll clothes
Clothespins and rope
Stethoscope
Rug
Magazine pictures
Refrigerator carton, large (to be used as a playhouse)

Art (Approximate total cost, $75.)

4 packages colored
  construction paper (100
  sheets, assorted colors)
Newsprint paper
Manila paper
Bogus art paper
Shelf paper
Colored tissue paper

Large container of crayons
15 small packages of crayons
White and colored chalk
School pencils
Felt tip markers (washable)
2 pairs large scissors
  (for teacher)
Small scissors (including
  some left-handed)

White glue
Paste
Scotch tape
Masking tape
Twine

Shirt cardboards
Tongue depressors
Paper plates
Art pipe cleaners
Straws
Clothespins
Glitter
Seeds (corn, lima beans,
  kidney beans)
Toothpicks
Wax paper

Scraps of yarn
Stapler
Rubber bands
Paper clips
Paper punch
Compass

Powder paint (1-lb. tins of
  red, yellow, blue, black,
  white)
Frozen juice cans
Brushes (5 each of #134,
  #AA3, #111)
Old shirts for smocks

Liquid starch (mix with
  powder paint for finger
  paint)
Soap flakes
Liquid detergent

Two 5-lb. bags of flour
One 5-lb. bag of canning salt
Cooking oil

  Recipe for play dough:
  2 parts flour to 1 part salt.
  Add a little cooking oil and
  water to desired consistency.

Paper towels
1-lb. cotton batting
Set of food coloring
Macaroni shells
Egg cartons
Paper tubes

MUSICAL INSTRUMENTS

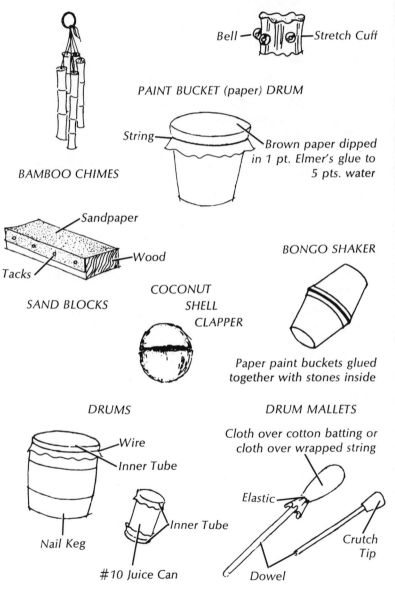

JINGLE CUFFS

Bell — Stretch Cuff

BAMBOO CHIMES

PAINT BUCKET (paper) DRUM

String

Brown paper dipped
in 1 pt. Elmer's glue to
5 pts. water

Sandpaper

Wood

Tacks

SAND BLOCKS

COCONUT
SHELL
CLAPPER

BONGO SHAKER

Paper paint buckets glued
together with stones inside

DRUMS

Wire

Inner Tube

Nail Keg

Inner Tube

#10 Juice Can

DRUM MALLETS

Cloth over cotton batting or
cloth over wrapped string

Elastic

Dowel

Crutch
Tip

Music (Approximate total cost, $125.)

Record player and records
Autoharp

Raw materials for homemade instruments:

6 cardboard paint buckets with lids	Sandpaper
	Coconuts
Nail keg	Nails
Dowels	Tin cans
White glue	Salt cartons
Wrapping paper	Scarves
Scrap pieces of wood	Flat elastic or knit cuffs
Bamboo (rug rollers)	Small bells
String	Inner tube, and
Rope	Wire

Some of the homemade instruments were:

Drums: paint bucket drums, tin can drums, nail keg drum	Coconut shell clappers
	Bamboo chimes
	Bamboo rattles
Drumsticks, mallets	Bongo shakers
Rhythm sticks	Stretch cuffs with bells
Tambourines	Sand blocks

BAMBOO RATTLES

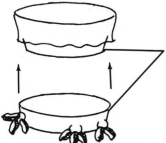

—Cork

Bamboo with stones or seeds inside

TAMBOURINE

Cut off paper paint buckets—one covered with brown paper dipped in glue mixture as above, second bucket placed over the first and bottle caps on wire loops added.

Science-related Materials (Approximate total cost, $15.)

ESS balance
ESS balance board
Lead sinkers
Rubbermaid Lazy Susan plus
  3' square Masonite top

Light bulbs #41 (flashlight)
Flashlight batteries
Copper wire
Lamp bases

Flashlights
Flexible mirrors (small
  squares backed with
  fabric)

Assorted colored transparent
  plastic sheets (20" x 24",
  from Gelatine Products Co.
  459 Adelphi St., Brooklyn,
  N.Y. 97938)
Assorted hand lenses and
  prisms
Dilutions tray and food
  colors and medicine
  droppers

Assorted magnets
Measuring sticks, assorted
  lengths

Woodworking (Approximate total cost, $50.)

*The scrap lumber used in this area will be useful in some
sand area projects.*

Work table
2 woodwork vises

Hack saws
Coping saws
Keyhole saw

2 hammers
Hand drill and set of bits
Combination pliers

Screwdrivers (small,
  medium, large)
Folding 6' rule
Assorted nails, tacks, and
  screws
Coarse and medium-coarse
  sandpaper
White glue
Twine

Scrap lumber and hardboard

ESS BALANCE

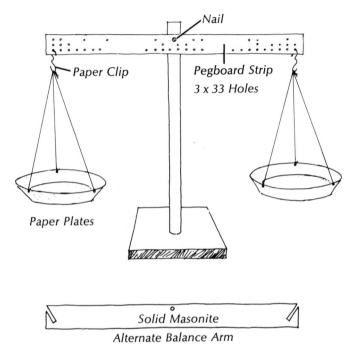

Nail

Paper Clip

Pegboard Strip
3 x 33 Holes

Paper Plates

Solid Masonite
Alternate Balance Arm

ESS 4-FOOT BALANCE BOARD

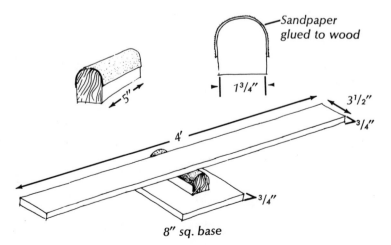

Sandpaper
glued to wood

5"

1³/₄"

4'

3¹/₂"

³/₄"

³/₄"

8" sq. base

Outdoor Equipment (Approximate total cost, $260.)

Many of the items listed under sand can be used outside as well.

2 8′ all-purpose boards
(Child Craft, 155 East 23 St.,
N.Y. 10010)
Ladder box (Child Craft)
2 nesting bridges (Child
Craft)
2 high (24″) sawhorses
(Child Craft)

2 low (12″) sawhorses
(Child Craft)
Refrigerator shipping box,
cardboard
Large wooden reel from
cable or rope
$1/2$″ rope
Outside balls
ESS walking board

Pumping Station (ESS) consists of:

Single tub (Sears Roebuck)
Jumbo size tub (see water
section)
Kitchen force pump

Stool to mount pump
50′ hose
Assorted hose connectors
and nozzles

SUPPLEMENTARY READING

SUPPLEMENTARY READING

The articles and essays presented in this book are but a sampling of the writings on open education. The following selection of books, articles, pamphlets, and films has been prepared for readers who wish to continue their exploration of this philosophy and the classroom practices associated with it.

The listing has been adapted from A Bibliography of Open Education *by Roland S. Barth and Charles H. Rathbone (see below).*

Allen, Marjorie. *Planning for Play*. Cambridge, Mass.: MIT Press, 1968.
A well-illustrated consideration of the meaning of play as manifested in the design of playgrounds. An impressive study.

Barth, Roland S. "On Selecting Materials for the Classroom," *Childhood Education,* vol. 47, no. 6, March, 1971.
Mr. Barth proposes—and discusses the implication of—five principles for selecting classroom materials.

_____. "Teaching: The Way It Is, The Way It Could Be," *Grade Teacher,* vol. 8, no. 4, Jan., 1970.
A comparison of the assumptions about children, learning, and knowledge underlying "most schools" with those underlying open schools and a discussion of the implications of the latter for the role of the teacher.

_____. "When Children Enjoy School: Some Lessons from Britain," *Childhood Education,* vol. 46, no. 4, Jan., 1970.
A description of characteristics of open schools that seem to be associated with children's enjoyment of school and a discussion of some of the problems that arise when children do enjoy school.

_____, and Charles H. Rathbone. *A Bibliography of Open Education*. Newton, Mass.: Early Childhood Education Study, 1971. (55 Chapel St., Newton, Mass. 02160, $1.25.)
A comprehensive, annotated, and categorized listing of articles, books, and films pertaining to open education.

Bernstein, Basil. "The Open School," *Where* (Supplement #12), 1967. (Advisory Centre for Education, 57 Russell St., Cambridge, England.)
Viewing schools as complex social organizations, Professor Bernstein, applying Durkheim, suggests two classifications: open (or organic) and closed (mechanical). The open school, emphasizing differences among children, educates for breadth not depth. It sees knowledge as uncompartmentalized and teachers as problem-posers rather than solution-givers. Its pedagogy allows for exploration of principles, not merely the memorization of standard operations; hence its boundaries seem ever flexible. This article offers an interesting point from which to view open education.

Big Rock Candy Mountain (periodical). Portola Institute. (1115 Merrill St., Menlo Park, Calif. 94025; yearly subscription: $8.)
Published six times per year, *Big Rock Candy Mountain* is an educational offshoot of the *Whole Earth Catalog*. It presents a fascinating variety of educational materials, all thoroughly reviewed and illustrated.

Biggs, Edith E., and James R. MacLean. *Freedom to Learn: An Active Learning Approach to Mathematics*. Don Mills: Addison-Wesley (Canada) Ltd., 1969. (57 Gervais Drive, Don Mills, Ontario.)
An important, handsomely illustrated book for teachers—and for teacher educators—written by the Assistant Superintendent of Curriculum for the Ontario Department of Education and Edith Biggs, H.M.I., who is Staff Inspector for Mathematics. Of special interest is their analysis of the roles of the teacher and principal as well as their description of in-service workshop programs.

Blackie, John. *Inside the Primary School*. London: Her Majesty's Stationery Office, 1967, paper. (In U.S.A., Pendragon House Inc., 1093 Charter Ave., Redwood City, Calif. 94063.) Written for laymen and parents by a former Chief Inspector of Schools, this comprehensive overview of primary schools places recent developments in clear historical perspective. It includes chapters on the different subject areas.

Brearley, Molly, ed. *The Teaching of Young Children: Some Applications of Piaget's Learning Theory*. New York: Schocken Books, 1970.
Miss Brearley and six of her colleagues at the Froebel Educational Institute describe successful school practice in the context of a carefully elaborated theory of learning. An important, useful book.

Brown, Mary, and Norman Precious, *The Integrated Day in the Primary School*. London: Ward Lock Educational, 1968.
A very practical account of "integrated day" activity, written by two Leicestershire heads. Appendices contain a bibliography and lists of suggested equipment. Illustrated.

Burgess, Lowery. *Fragments: A Way of Seeing, A Way of Seeking*. Newton: Education Development Center, 1970. (55 Chapel Street, Newton, Mass. 02160.)
A curious collection of activity cards "primarily concerned," writes the author, "with the boundaries of experience." Though originally conceived for a high school visual education course, many are appropriate for younger children. Imaginative and amusing.

Bussis, Anne M., and Edward A. Chittenden. *Analysis of an Approach to Open Education*. Princeton, N.J.: Educational Testing Service, 1970.
The interim report of a study conducted by Educational Testing Service in cooperation with participants in the Follow Through Program of Education Development Center. It seeks to clarify a theoretical framework for viewing open education. Special attention is given to examining the teacher's work in the open education setting. An impressive, helpful document.

Cass, Joan, and D.E.M. Gardner. *The Role of the Teacher in the Infant and Nursery School*. London: Pergamon Press, 1965.
The authors selected eighteen nursery school teachers and thirty infant school teachers each of whom was judged to represent "good," i.e., open education, teaching practices.

After the teachers had been observed for 180 minutes, their classroom behavior was separated into eighty categories, and the frequency of each behavior noted. The intent of Miss Cass and Miss Gardner was ". . . to show what constitutes good and successful teaching in informal education."

Charbonneau, Manon P. *Learning to Think in a Math Lab.* Boston: National Association of Independent Schools, April, 1971. (4 Liberty Square, Boston, Mass. 02109; $2.50.)
Primarily concerned with the learning needs of nine-, ten- and eleven-year-olds, this monograph describes very specifically how a teacher organized, equipped, and maintained an activity-centered math lab. Illustrated.

Cazden, Courtney, B. *Infant School.* Newton: Education Development Center, 1969. (55 Chapel St., Newton, Mass. 02160, 50¢.)
The transcription of Dr. Cazden's 1967 interview with Miss Susan M. Williams, Director of Gordonbrock Infant School in London. Produced by Adeline Naiman. Illustrated.

Clegg, A. B., ed. *The Excitement of Writing,* London: Chatto & Windus (Educational) Ltd., 1966.
A remarkable collection of writing by children from the economically depressed mining communities of the West Riding. Included are some suggestions by their teachers on ways of encouraging good writing—suggestions that rule out the use of drills and exercises, substituting in their stead methods more in keeping with the approaches of open education. The editor, long-time Chief Education Officer for the district, presents a convincing case against external examinations, which have for so long dictated uniform "standards" by which writing is judged, as he comments on recent curriculum changes in junior school English.

Cohen, David K. "Children and their Primary Schools: Volume II," *Harvard Educational Review,* vol. 38, no. 2, Spring, 1968. (Editorial Offices, Longfellow Hall, Cambridge, Mass. 02138, $1.)
A critical review of The Plowden Report's research component, volume II.

Consultative Committee on the Primary School. *The Hadow Report: A Report of the Consultative Committee on the Primary School.* London: Her Majesty's Stationery Office, 1931 (reprinted 1962). (In U.S.A., Pendragon House Inc., 1093 Charter Ave., Redwood City, Calif. 94063.)
The oft-referred to precursor of The Plowden Report, a wide-ranging survey of primary school children and the way they grow, their teachers, and their schools, including reports on administrative matters, the situation of the retarded child, examinations and their effects, curriculum offerings, etc.

Cox, C. B., and A. E. Dyson. *Black Paper Two.* London: Critical Quarterly Society, 1969. (The Secretary, Critical Quarterly Society, 2 Radcliffe Ave., London, N.W. 10.)
A collection of essays published to stem the tide of progressivism in England. The section on open education rather angrily debunks "discovery" methods, modern math, and informal approaches in the early grades; it is entitled, "Primary Schools: Moving Progressively Backwards."

_____. *Fight for Education.* London: Critical Quarterly Society, 1969. (The Secretary, Critical Quarterly Society, 2 Radcliffe Ave., London, N.W. 10.)
Subtitled, "A Black Paper," this collection of nearly twenty essays was presented to every Member of Parliament in reaction to recent "progressive" trends in British education.

Dean, Joan. *Art and Craft in the Primary School Today,* 2nd ed. London: A. & C. Black, 1970.
A detailed, illustrated consideration of a number of practical techniques for art and craft work.

Department of Education and Science. *Evelyn Lowe Primary School, London* (Building Bulletin #36). London: Her Majesty's Stationery Office, 1967. (In U.S.A., Pendragon House Inc., 1093 Charter Ave., Redwood City, Calif. 94063.) The thoughtful account of how a specially appointed Development Group set about planning for this inner-London primary school. Illustrated and jargon-free.

Early Childhood Education Study. *I Am Here Today* (film). 43½ min., b&w. Newton: Education Development Center, May

1969. (EDC Film Library, 55 Chapel Street, Newton, Mass. 02160; purchase: $215; rental: $10.)
A morning visit to an open classroom at Shady Hill School, Cambridge, Massachusetts. Composed of five-, six- and seven-year olds, this class operates on a highly individualized basis. Betsye Sargent and her two assistants have developed a format that allows the older children to act as teachers of the younger ones while still being free to follow their individual interests.

_____. *Materials: A Useful List of Classroom Items That Can Be Scrounged or Purchased.* Newton: Education Development Center, 1970. (55 Chapel Street, Newton, Mass. 02160; 50¢.)
A useful seventeen-page list of free or inexpensive materials, including addresses of suppliers.

_____. *Three Year Olds* (film). 10–30 min., b&w. Newton: Education Development Center, 1970. (EDC Film Library, 55 Chapel Street, Newton, Mass. 02160; rental: $10.)
Conceived as "ethological," these nine short films offer an unedited "real time" view of the interactions of preschoolers as seen through the subjective eye of the cameraman. Filmed by Allan Leitman at the City and Country School in New York.

Educational Facilities Lab. *Room To Learn* (film). 22 min., color. (Available from Association Films; purchase: $125, rental: free.)
A film of the Early Learning Center of Stamford, Connecticut, where the principles of open education have affected the physical environment of a specially designed building for pre-schoolers.

Elementary Science Study. *The ESS Reader.* Newton: Education Development Center, 1971. (55 Chapel St., Newton, Mass. 02160.)
A collection of working papers that convey the philosophy and general approach of the ESS staff. The introduction is written by David Hawkins, who served as Director of ESS during its formative years.

Engstrom, Georgianna, ed. *Open Education: The Legacy of the Progressive Movement* (pamphlet). Washington, D.C.: National Association for the Education of Young Children, 1970.

(1834 Connecticut Ave., N.W., Washington, D.C. 20009, $2.)
A conference report that includes papers by David Elkind,
James B. Macdonald, Roma Gans, Vincent R. Rogers, and
Bernard Spodek.

Farmer, Irene. "Experimental Schools," *Forum,* vol. 11, no. 3,
Summer, 1969.
A critical review of Brown and Precious *The Integrated Day in
The Primary School,* which takes the authors especially to task
for their bland, all-inclusive conceptualization of "integrated."

Featherstone, Joseph. "Experiments in Learning," *The New
Republic,* vol. 159, no. 24, December 14, 1968.
Describing how reading and writing are learned in the better
junior schools of England, Mr. Featherstone paraphrases the
finest teachers as saying that, "Children write for people they
trust; they don't write freely until they can talk with confidence; and, except for the work of certain born storytellers,
most of their best writing comes from things they experience
directly." When a teacher pays serious attention to the context of the child's writing, he contends, a bond of interest
unites that teacher and the child; motivated by that bond
and not by grades or spelling *per se,* the child will inevitably
come to care about the precision with which he communicates and will attend to the mechanics of the writing in due
course. When children write on subjects of their own choosing and are confident of a concerned adult as their audience,
the ensuing work is likely to be sincere and lively, unencum-
bered by stock phrases and conventional truisms.

———. "The Primary School Revolution in Britain," *The New
Republic,* 1967. (1244 19th St., N.W., Washington, D.C. 20036,
50¢.)
This collection of three 1967 articles by Mr. Featherstone has
for good reason probably received the widest circulation of
any printed material dealing with British primary education.

———. "Schools for Learning," *The New Republic,* vol. 159,
no. 25–26, December 21, 1968.
On the teaching of mathematics at the junior school level,
including commentary on the use of concrete materials,
evaluation and procedures for recording student progress,

192

spatial and temporal reorganization of classrooms necessitated by a changing, problem-oriented curriculum, and the special strengths and skills demanded of teachers who elect to teach this way.

_____. *Schools Where Children Learn.* New York: Liveright, 1971.
A collection of articles that appeared over several years in *The New Republic.* Though emphasizing recent trends in British primary education, Mr. Featherstone has also included pieces on day care centers, street academies, and the Talent Corps as well as some film and book reviews.

Felt, Henry. *Choosing to Learn* (film). 25 min., color, Newton: Education Development Center, 1970. (55 Chapel St., Newton, Mass. 02160; rental: $10.)
Depicts life in the World of Inquiry School, an experimental Title III demonstration project in Rochester, New York. Most striking is a scene of a ten-year-old welding under the tutelage of a retired welder, now serving as a part-time teacher aide.

_____. *Medbourne Primary School: Four Days in May* (film). Newton: Education Development Center, 1970. (55 Chapel St., Newton, Mass. 02160; rental: $10.)
The documentation of classroom life within an excellent rural primary school in Leicestershire.

Follow Through Program. *Instructional Aids, Materials, and Supplies.* Newton: Education Development Center, 1970. (55 Chapel Street, Newton, Mass. 02160; $1.)
A 75-page list of possible curriculum materials for an open classroom compiled by the staff of the EDC Follow Through Program who consult with public schools across the country.

Forum (periodical). Leicester: University of Leicester School of Education. (86 Headland Rd., Evington, Leicester, LE56AD, England.)
A British periodical published three times a year "for the discussion of new trends in education." Brian Simon, editor.

Gardner, D. E. M. *Experiment and Tradition in Primary Schools.* London: Methuen & Co., Ltd., 1966. (In U.S.A., Barnes & Noble.)

193

Miss Gardner, a leader in child development at the University of London's Institute of Education, in three longitudinal studies spanning nearly a quarter of a century, has favorably compared the attitudes and achievements of Engilsh children in open education schools with their counterparts in traditional primary schools. This represents, along with sections of The Plowden Report, a rare attempt at serious, rigorous research on the differential effects of this type of schooling.

Gibbons, Maurice. "What is Individualized Instruction?" *Interchange,* vol. 1, no. 2, 1970. (Ontario Institute for Studies in Education, 252 Bloor St. West, Toronto.)
Professor Gibbons of Simon Fraser University presents a useful analysis of factors contributing to (and in many instances defining) "individualization." The open education classroom is one of several educational environments he then considers in detail.

Grannis, Joseph C. "The School as a Model of Society" *Harvard Graduate School of Education Association Bulletin,* vol. 12, no. 2, Fall, 1967. (Publications Office, Harvard Graduate School of Education, Cambridge, Mass. 02138, 55¢.)
Asserting that the structure of school itself instructs students, Dr. Grannis looks at three alternative models: the "factory" school, the "corporation" school, and the open education or "family" school.

Gross, Beatrice and Ronald. "A Little Bit of Chaos," *Saturday Review,* vol. 53, no. 20, May 16, 1970.
A broad, helpful overview of the open education movement in this country, by the co-editors of *Radical School Reform.*

Harkins, John. *Box Breaking* (pamphlet). Philadelphia: Friends Committee on Education, Nov., 1969. (1515 Cherry St., Philadelphia, Pa. 19102, 75¢.)
An informal report of a summer Workshop in Creative Education for teachers wishing to "loosen up" their classrooms. A film, entitled *Side Streets,* was also produced in connection with this workshop.

Hawkins, David. "Square Two, Square Three." *Forum,* vol. 12, no. 1, Autumn, 1969.

Calling for additional theoretical work to support and strengthen recent advances in open education practice, Professor Hawkins raises difficult questions regarding such issues as the distinction between "authoritarian" and "permissive," children's selectiveness during the assimilation of culture, teachers' diagnostic problems, and the relationship of primary schools to secondary.

Hawkins, Frances P. *The Logic of Action*. Boulder: University of Colorado, 1969. (Elementary Science Advisory Center, 603 Ketchum, University of Colorado, Boulder, Colo., $3.00.)
The perceptive account of work with six children in a Colorado public school. Although the children were very young (four years old) and deaf, Mrs. Hawkins' commentary on more general issues—such as how the personalities of individual children affect how (and often what) those children learn, the challenges teachers face as they seek to extend the understanding of individual minds, various institutional hindrances to learning, and problems of evaluation—seem broadly relevant. Her observations "illustrate, and perhaps help to elaborate, an essential principle of learning: that given a rich environment—with open-end 'raw' materials—children can be encouraged and trusted to take a large part in the design of their own learning, and that with this encouragement and trust they can learn well." Illustrated with photographs of the children at work.

Hegeler, Sten, *Choosing Toys For Children*. London: Tavistock Publications, 1963. (11 New Fetter Lane, London E.C. 4.)
An interesting, easily read little book containing: a brief history of toys and ideas of play; a discussion of important developmental characteristics of children 1–12; an appendix listing different toys, cataloged according to price and appropriate age. Of particular interest is the thoughtful introduction by D. E. M. Gardner in which she discusses the nature of play and the difference between play and work for the child, and a chapter by the author, "Some Problems of Play and Toys," in which he considers why children play, the distinction between play and work, etc.

Hollamby, Lillian. *Young Children Living and Learning*. London: Longmans, Green, 1962.

A realistic, sympathetic guide to teaching in an informal infant school, written by the Principal of Alnwick College of Education in Northumberland. Practical, yet based on solid understanding of the ways in which children learn.

Holt, John. *How Children Fail.* New York: Pitman, 1964. (Also Dell paperback.)
The earliest and perhaps most influential book by this well-known advocate of student-directed learning.

_____. *How Children Learn.* New York: Pitman, 1967. (Also Dell paperback.)
Anecdotal accounts of children learning; much direct observation, combined with thoughtful speculation about the learning process as exhibited both in and out of school.

_____. *What Do I Do Monday?* New York: Dutton, 1970.
A practical guide for teachers wishing to "loosen up" their classrooms.

I/D/E/A. *The British Infant School: Report of an International Seminar* (pamphlet). Melbourne, Fla.: Institute for Development of Educational Activities, Inc., 1969. (Box 446, Melbourne, Fla.. 32901, $1.)
A profusely illustrated occasional paper reporting a seminar held in England in 1969. It includes position statements by Miss E. Marianne Parry, former Inspector of Infant and Nursery Schools in Bristol, and by Lady Bridget Plowden, Chairman of the Central Advisory Council for Education.

_____. *Primary Education in England: The English Infant School* (film). 17 min., color. Melbourne, Fla.: I/D/E/A, 1969. (Information and Services Division, Box 446, Melbourne, Fla. 32901; purchase: $120; rental: $10.)
Shows open education at work in the Sea Mills Infant School in Bristol, England. Directed by John Patterson.

James, Charity. *Young Lives at Stake: A Reappraisal of Secondary Schools.* London: Collins, 1968.
Mrs. James, Director of the Goldsmiths' College Curriculum Laboratory at the University of London, turns her attention to the implications of an open education-like approach for British secondary education.

Judson, Madison E. *Books of Interest Concerning Infant, Primary and Elementary Schools in the United States and in England.* Boston: School Services Group, 1969. (48 Clark St., Belmont, Mass. 02140, $1.)
A bibliography of over 400 entries, compiled by the former headmaster of the Fayerweather Street School in Cambridge, Mass. It includes an introduction by Dan Pinck, Director of the School Services Group in Boston.

Kohl, Herbert R. *The Open Classroom.* New York: New York Review/Vintage, 1970.
Subtitled, "A Practical Guide to a New Way of Teaching," this short book gives advice to the practitioner who wishes to "loosen up" his classroom while remaining within the public school setting.

Lawrence, Evelyn, ed. *Friedrich Froebel and English Education.* London: Routledge and Kegan Paul, 1952 (republished 1969).
A collection of essays considering Froebel's contributions to British Primary Education, with chapters on the origins of the kindergarten, his influence on primary and preparatory school practices, the religious roots of his philosophy, and a general overview of the Froebel movement in England. Nathan Isaacs' essay, "Froebel's Educational Philosophy in 1952," relates basic Froebelian doctrine to the freedom espoused by adherents of open education.

Leitman, Allan. *Another Way to Learn* (film). 12 min., b&w. Newton: Early Childhood Education Study, 1967. (55 Chapel St., Newton, Mass. 02160; rental: $10.)
Nancy Howe's first-grade classroom depicts open education in action in Wellesley, Mass.

———. *They Can Do It* (film). 33 min., b&w. Newton: Early Childhood Education Study, 1968. (55 Chapel St., Newton, Mass. 02160; rental: $10.)
The director of the Early Childhood Education Study at Education Development Center documents the development that transpires over the span of one year within a first-grade classroom taught by Lovie Glen in Philadelphia.

Marsh, Leonard. *Alongside the Child: Experiences in Primary School.* London: A. & C. Black; New York: Praeger, 1970.
A detailed account of teaching in an open setting. Illustrated.

Marshall, Sybil. *Adventure in Creative Education.* London and New York: Pergamon Press, Ltd., 1968.
The narration of Mrs. Marshall's work with mature, experienced primary teachers in a twelve-week workshop course. With the intention of placing "each teacher for a short time in the position of the thought that he should again know what it [feels] like to be a child faced with all kinds of demands made on him," she put her sixteen teachers through a variety of imaginative experiences. Throughout, she had three aims: "The first was to place the teacher as often as possible in the position of the child; the second was to ask him personally to attempt as many creative activities as possible; and the third was to give him a taste of learning as an integrated whole."

_____. *An Experiment in Education.* Cambridge: Cambridge University Press, 1963.
A compelling, autobiographical account of Mrs. Marshall's work at the Kingston County Primary School in Cambridgeshire, during the course of which she evolved an informal, activity-oriented teaching style. Handsomely illustrated.

Mason, Stewart C., ed. *In Our Experience.* London: Longmans, Green, 1970.
A collection of essays chronicling change as it has occurred in the schools of Leicestershire County, edited by Leicestershire's long-time Director of Education.

Mathematical Association. *Primary Mathematics: A Further Report.* London: G. Bell & Sons, Ltd., 1970.
A follow-up to the Mathematical Association's earlier publication, *The Teaching of Mathematics in Primary Schools,* this handbook for teachers presents, in a very detailed fashion, concepts and techniques appropriate to primary school mathematics. Illustrated.

Ministry of Education. *Village Schools* (Building Bulletin 3). London: Her Majesty's Stationery Office, 1961. (In U.S.A.,

Pendragon House Inc., 1093 Charter Ave., Redwood City, Calif. 94063.)
An architecturally-oriented study of rural primary schools, with emphasis on the organization of space and furniture but including some discussion of open education rationale. Illustrated.

Ministry of Education and Central Office of Information, *Moving and Growing: Physical Education in the Primary School, Part One and Part Two.* London: Her Majesty's Stationery Office, 1952. (In U.S.A., Pendragon House Inc., 1093 Charter Ave. Redwood City, Calif. 94063.)
A common-sense consideration of what it means to move —physical movement as a means and as an indication of human development. Discussion of games, dances, throwing and skipping; the role of repetition, versatility, fluency; recognition of maturity, mood, style and character through observation of natural movement; the stages of growth and dexterity. Thoroughly illustrated. Though not particularly concerned with recent reforms in primary education, this book does indicate one important, long-standing concern of infant teachers and thus provides an important background against which to view recent changes in British schools.

Minuchin, Patricia, Barbara Biber, Edna Shapiro, and Herbert Zimiles. *The Psychological Impact of School Experience.* New York: Basic Books, 1969.
The most extensive and most rigorous study yet attempted in the United States comparing the different effects that "traditional" and "modern" schooling have on the intellectual and social learning of grade school children.

Murrow, Casey and Liza. *Children Come First: The Inspired Work of English Primary Schools.* New York: American Heritage Press, 1971.
A sympathetic overview by two young Americans who spent a year in England observing in open education classrooms. They include considerable (non-technical) detail of what life is like for a child in this environment. The book concludes with a list of schools visited and a brief bibliography.

National Froebel Foundation. *Froebel Pamphlets*. (2 Manchester Square, London, W 1.)

A series of short pamphlets written for teachers on various aspects of primary school education. The following entry represents an example.

————. *Some Aspects of Piaget's Work*. London: National Froebel Foundation, 1955 (reprinted 1966). A pamphlet containing three essays: "Children's Ideas of Number," by Evelyn Lawrence and T. R. Theakston, "The Wider Significance of Piaget's Work," by Nathan Isaacs, and "Piaget and Progressive Education," also by Mr. Isaacs.

New Schools Exchange Newsletter (periodical). (2840 Hidden Valley Lane, Santa Barbara, Calif. 93103; yearly subscription: $10.)

This fortnightly newsletter contains descriptions of radical and experimental schools in the United States. It also carries information about people seeking schools and schools seeking people.

Occasional Papers. Early Childhood Education Study, (55 Chapel St., Newton, Mass. 02160, $1.)

A series of articles of interest to Head Start and elementary school teachers, many of which appear sympathetic to the principles of open education.

Outlook (periodical). Mountain View Center for Environmental Education. (University of Colorado, 1441 Broadway, Boulder, Colo. 80302.)

Staff members for 1970–1971 included David and Francis Hawkins, Anthony Kallet, Elwyn Richardson, and others—all deeply committed to the philosophy of open education.

Pearce, Lucia. "Exploration-Innovation: The New Learning Environment." *The Science Teacher,* vol. 36, no. 2, Feb., 1969. Searching for a structured environment that is truly an "extension of the learner" (rather than of the teacher), Mrs. Pearce sketches out the requirements of a studio-lab "free learning environment," one that emphasizes a certain teacher role (mediator, resource, catalyst), the mixed grouping of children, flexible spatial arrangements (including modular furniture the children themselves can assemble), considerable choice for children in what and when and how they learn—all with the goal of fostering autonomous, independent, "self-actualizing" behavior in young children.

Peters, R. S., ed. *Perspective on Plowden*. London: Routledge and Kegan Paul, 1969.
A selection of essays concerning the child-centered primary school education described in The Plowden Report. Written by faculty of London University's Institute of Education, these articles have provided a theoretical foundation for critical attacks on open education in England.

Plowden, Lady Bridget et al. *Children and their Primary Schools: A Report of the Central Advisory Council for Education*. London: Her Majesty's Stationery Office, 1966. (In U.S.A., Pendragon House Inc., 1093 Charter Ave., Redwood City, Calif. 94063. vol. I, $5.; vol. II, $6.50.)
The most comprehensive (and politically significant) discussion to date of the rationale as well as the practices of modern British primary schools. Volume I is the main body of the report; volume II consists in the main of statistical tables, though several of its appendices (such as those dealing with the education of gypsies, school management, and the effects of streaming) may be of general interest.

Razzell, Arthur. *Juniors: A Postscript to Plowden*. Aylesbury: Penguin Books, Ltd., 1968.
An historical account of recent post-Plowden developments in England's junior schools, addressed mainly to parents. Comparable to Blackie's book on the primary schools, this paperback describes what the new junior schools look like inside and out, and attempts to account for recent changes.

Richardson, Elwin S. *In the Early World*. Wellington: New Zealand Council of Educational Research, 1964; New York: Pantheon, 1969.
An exciting account of Richardson's school in Oruaiti in northern New Zealand. Handsomely illustrated in color, it contains chapters on mathematics, nature study, techniques to establish awareness, the place of values in the development

201

of children, etc. Although apparently developed independently of the current movement in British primary education, Richardson's school shows remarkable affinity to the best of these practices.

Ridgeway, Lorna, and Irene Lawton. *Family Grouping in the Primary School,* 2nd ed. London: Ward Lock Educational, 1968.
A thorough consideration of the means and objectives of multi-age or vertical grouping. Illustrated and concludes with a useful bibliography.

Rogers, Vincent R. "A Macrocosmic Approach to Inquiry," *Social Education,* vol. 34, no. 1, Jan., 1970.
A look at the principles underlying the inquiry approach to social studies curriculum, including an analysis of the recent revolution in British primary education and its implicit rationale.

————, ed. "Primary Education in England: An Interview with John Coe," *Phi Delta Kappan,* vol. 52, no. 9, May, 1971.
An interview with Oxfordshire's Chief Advisor for Primary Schools.

————, ed. *Teaching in the British Primary School.* New York: Macmillan, 1970.
A useful collection of essays, both on general topics and on specific curriculum areas, written by British practitioners and edited by Professor Rogers of the University of Connecticut.

Sargent, Betsye. *The Integrated Day in an American School* (pamphlet). Boston: National Association of Independent Schools, 1970. (4 Liberty Square, Boston, Mass. 02109, $2.50.)
These notes, made by an experienced teacher from the Shady Hill School in Cambridge, convey very concretely and on a day-to-day basis what it means to run an open education classroom in the United States. Edward Yeomans has written the foreword.

Schneir, Walter and Miriam, "The Joy of Learning—In the Open Corridor," *New York Times Magazine,* April 4, 1971.
A description of P.S. 84 and other "open corridor" classrooms

in New York, including a chronicle of their origin under the sponsorship of Mrs. Lillian Weber.

Schools Council for Curriculum and Examinations. *Mathematics in Primary Schools* (Curriculum Bulletin #1.), 2nd ed. London: Her Majesty's Stationery Office, 1966 (In U.S.A., Pendragon House Inc., 1093 Charter Ave., Redwood City, Calif. 94063.)
Though mostly concerned with the details of teaching mathematics, this thorough pamphlet does attempt to place current reforms in that subject area within the broad context of the changing pattern of primary school education throughout England. It attends, also, to recent research on how children learn and provides a concise summary of the studies of Piaget. Prepared by Edith Biggs, H.M.I.

Schools Council/Ford Foundation Anglo-American Primary Education Project. *Informal Schools in Britain Today.* London: Macmillian Education Ltd.; New York: Citation Press, 1971 and 1972.
A series of 23 booklets describing and analyzing successful practice of informal schooling. Titles include: "The Government of Education" by Maurice Kogan; "Towards Informality" by J. M. Pullan; "The Headteacher's Role" by Ann Cook and Herb Mack; "From Home to School" by A. L. Murton; "A Junior School" by H. J. Probert and Christopher Jarman; "Trends in School Design" by Eric Pearson; "Art" by Henry Pluckrose; "Informal Reading and Writing" by J. E. Johnson and Joan Tamburrini; "Evaluation of Achievement" by Douglas Pidgeon, and two booklets on teaching mathematics by Edith Biggs.

Shanker, Albert. "The 'Open Classroom' Concept." *New York Times,* Jan. 24, 1971.
In the weekly *New York Times* column sponsored by the United Federation of Teachers, the president of that organization reviews Charles Silberman's *Crisis in the Classroom.* Following a general statement in support of the "open classroom" idea, Mr. Shanker goes on to elaborate three basic points: "First, we must recognize that there is no single method which is best for all teachers and for all students.

203

Second, the evidence now available does not prove that the open classroom produces greater achievement in reading and math. Third, the techniques of the open classroom cannot be easily adopted by every teacher."

Silberman, Charles E. *Crisis in the Classroom.* New York: Random House, 1970. (Also Vintage paperback.)
In this comprehensive review of American public education, the result of a three-and-one-half year study commissioned by the Carnegie Corporation, Mr. Silberman takes a careful, enthusiastic look at the British infant school as a model for reform of elementary education in the United States.

Thackery, John, Juanita Chaudhry, and Dorothea Grine. *Open Door* (pamphlet). New York: Center for Urban Education, 1970. (105 Madison Avenue, New York, N.Y. 10016. $1.50.)
An illustrated description of the "open door" and "open corridor" work of Mrs. Lillian Weber and her colleagues in New York's P.S. 123 and P.S. 84.

Tobier, Arthur J. "The Open Classroom: Humanizing the Coldness of Public Places." *The Center Forum,* vol. 3, no. 6, May 1969.
An account of Lillian Weber's work to establish a well-equipped, family-grouped "open corridor" in Harlem's P.S. 123.

Ulin, Donald S. "What I Learned from the British Schools," *Grade Teacher,* vol. 86, no. 6, February 1969.
A sixth-grade teacher's thoughtful account of a sabbatical year spent in several Leicestershire schools. After describing the classrooms he visited, Mr. Ulin offers, subject by subject, his impression of how British pupils compare with their American counterparts. He also offers some criticism of both American and English schools.

Vermont State Department of Education. *Vermont Design for Education.* Montpelier: State Department of Education, n.d.
The articulation of seventeen premises that, taken in summation "constitute a goal, an ideal, a student-centered philosophy for the process of education in Vermont," followed by a consideration of several suggested strategies for implementa-

tion of those ideals. In all, a remarkable expression of commitment by a state agency to the principles of open education.

Walberg, Herbert J., and Susan Christie Thomas. *Characteristics of Open Education: Toward an Operational Definition.* Newton: TDR Associates, Inc., May, 1971. (375 Elliot Street, Newton, Mass. 02164.)

This study, commissioned by the Pilot Communities Program of Education Development Center, has sought "1) to analyze the concept of open education; 2) to find its essential features; 3) to develop explicit, specific, concrete indicators of each feature; and 4) to check the validity of the indicators with the major writings on the subject, and with important theorists and practitioners in Great Britain and the United States." An important and helpful document, one that includes "Appendix A—Quotations from Major Writings" and "Appendix D— Pedagogical Characteristics of Open Education Teachers at the Primary Level."

Walter, Marion, and Stephen Brown. "What If Not." *Mathematics Teaching,* no. 46, Spring, 1969.

Noting how most math courses emphasize the need to arrive at final, polished products to the neglect of any stress on problem-posing, the authors present work on geoboards as a means of helping both students and teachers to generate new ways of thinking about mathematics.

Weber, Lillian. *The English Infant School and Informal Education.* Englewood Cliffs, N.J.: Prentice-Hall, 1971.

A comprehensive study by a CCNY Professor of Early Childhood Education who recently spent eighteen months in England studying the organization, program, and philosophy of British infant schools.

————. *Infants School* (film). 32 min., b&w. Newton: Education Development Center. (EDC Film Library, 55 Chapel Street, Newton, Mass. 02160; purchase: $125; rental: $10.)

Almost unedited portrayal of activity in London's Gordonbrock Infant School, concentrating on children's movement in the classroom. For a transcription of an interview with Miss Susan Williams, headmistress of this school, see Cazden's *Infant School* pamphlet. Filmed by Peter Theobald.

Whole Earth Catalog (periodical). Portola Institute. (1115 Merrill St., Menlo Park, Calif. 94025; yearly subscription: $8.) A delightful compendium of tools, equipment, catalogs, and books, published twice a year by Stewart Brand. Four supplements are also issued annually, $1.)

Yeomans, Edward. *Education for Initiative and Responsibility* (pamphlet). Boston: National Association of Independent Schools, Nov. 1967. (4 Liberty Square, Boston, Mass. 02109, $1.)
Thoughtful comments on a visit to the schools of Leicestershire County in April, 1967, with special attention to describing and analyzing "integrated day" and "vertical grouping." Appendix III lists curriculum materials and equipment recommended for an open education classroom, including addresses of manufacturers.

ABOUT THE CONTRIBUTORS

ROLAND S. BARTH is Principal of Angier Elementary School in Newton, Massachusetts.

EDITH H. E. CHURCHILL has for a number of years been a staff member of the Elementary Science Study in Newton, Massachusetts. She is now an advisor in the Follow Through Project, also at Education Development Center.

DAVID HAWKINS, former Director of the Elementary Science Study, is presently Professor of Philosophy and Director of the Mountain View Center for Environmental Education at the University of Colorado in Boulder.

JOHN HOLT, author of *How Children Fail, How Children Learn, The Underachieving School* and *What Do I Do Monday?*, currently serves as consultant to the Fayerweather School of Cambridge, Massachusetts.

WILLIAM P. HULL, formerly associated with the Elementary Science Study, is now an Advisor to the Follow Through Project of Education Development Center in Newton, Massachusetts.

ANTHONY KALLET is an American-born psychologist who for several years served on the advisory staff of the Leicestershire Education Department in England. He is now on the staff of Mountain View Center for Environmental Education in Boulder, Colorado.

ALLAN LEITMAN, filmmaker, is presently Director of the Early Childhood Education Study at the Advisory for Open Education in Cambridge, Massachusetts.

CHARLES H. RATHBONE formerly Assistant Professor of Education at Oberlin College, now teaches in an open classroom in the Oberlin public schools.